EFFECTIVE CHANGE
Twenty ways to make it happen

Andrew Leigh is a senior partner in Maynard Leigh Associates and author of several other management books. He trained as an economist at the London School of Economics, has an MA in Manpower Studies and is a Fellow of the Institute of Personnel Management. He has extensive experience as a practising manager. As a senior partner in Maynard Leigh Associates, he provides consultancy and training to the company's clients. He can be contacted on 071-371 5288 or by fax on 071-371 5299.

EFFECTIVE CHANGE
Twenty ways to make it happen

Andrew Leigh

Institute of Personnel Management

For my sister Vivienne

First published 1988
Reprinted 1991 and 1994

Phototypeset by Illustrated Arts, Sutton, Surrey
and printed in Great Britain by Cromwell Press , Melksham, Wiltshire.

British Library Cataloguing in Publication Data

Leigh, Andrew
    Effective change.
    1. Personnel Management
    I. Title
    658.3

ISBN 0-85292-412-7

Contents

Acknowledgements

I should like to thank the following: Dr Jean Neumann of the Tavistock Institute of Human Relations who offered much appreciated encouragement and advice; John Nichol of the Work Research Unit; Bryan Stevens, Director of the Industrial Participation Association; *Community Care* magazine for permission to adapt material from two published articles of mine on Stress and Power; library staff of the Institute of Personnel Management and also the London Borough of Croydon; the London Borough of Croydon for permission to use material relating to the social services department; Macmillan Publishing Company for a review copy of *Thriving on Chaos* by Tom Peters; William Collins Sons & Company for a review copy of *Odyssey* by John Sculley; Bantam Press for a review copy of *The Renewal Factor* by Robert Waterman, Jr; Matthew Reisz for suggesting this book; my own management team for never failing to remind me that writing about management is not the same as doing it; my wife Gillian for her ever constant support and my two sons, Aiden and Darion, who cheered from the sidelines.

Introduction

So much is available on the subject of organizational change that a way must be found to help managers make sense of it all. When the draft of this book was finished, in addition to my own views it had generated a computerized data base of hundreds of extracts from numerous studies and a bibliography stretching into infinity.

As a practising manager I have experienced the bombardment of material about managing change. I too have puzzled at the often contradictory advice offered, the mixture of research and pearls of wisdom that flow like lava from a volcano.

When the precursor to this book – *20 Ways to Manage Better* – was published, it seemed necessary to offer some explanation for attempting to distil management wisdom into such brief form. Each of the 20 topics covered had its own army of experts and I felt it a little presumptuous to interpret their know-how into a few short pages. In the event, however, the formula proved popular. Even the IPM's Director somewhat shyly admitted in print that he had read it avidly! So *Effective Change* has been written on the familiar principle that if something works well, repeat it.

Most managers cause change, though not always for the better. Yet no one is interested in change for its own sake but because it produces tangible improvements of some kind. In this book, therefore, we are concerned with *positive* change, which builds an organization, develops its employees, and creates new opportunities for further positive change and development.

Attempts to manage organizational developments can be viewed either in terms of the dynamics of change following an intervention; or in terms of implementation, the activities which change agents must undertake to produce planned change. Since this book is primarily about implementation, it is divided into three sub groups, namely strategies, procedures and techniques. This classification is arbitrary, and strategy has been interpreted in the widest sense. There are also inevitable overlaps as some themes cut across several topics.

Like most managers I am willing to spend time learning about strategies, procedures and techniques only if they help me to do my own job better. That principle has guided the selection of material. In hacking my way through the dense undergrowth of work on organizational change I have been constrained and also helped by my own management role. The latter has provided a useful filter through which to sift potential advice and imposed strict limits on the depth of research. The information is here because it seems likely to be useful to working managers. Anything which could not be turned to practical use has been excluded.

Considering how much material is available on the subject of change it is surprising how hard it is to find dependable practical lessons to apply on the job. This can be symbolized by studies of leadership; after ploughing through all 700 pages of Stogdill's definitive and much respected *Handbook of Research on Leadership*, the only thing that becomes clear is that most of the findings contradict each other!

The real life experiences of managers, the captains of industry and successful entrepreneurs are perhaps slightly less inconsistent but frequently idiosyncratic. Their message is: 'I do it my way'. In selecting material I have generally refrained from bolstering the presentation with reassurances about overwhelming evidence or quoting endless sources which few managers have either the time or inclination to pursue. If it is here you can assume that there is usually a sound reason and you will only know if the advice works by trying it.

There are hundreds of organizational change methods available and *Effective Change* does not purport to cover them all, or be a totally representative selection. Instead it offers a route to gaining some of the basics about the subject and then deciding where else you want to travel. There is no instant, packaged answer to managing change and this book, for all its deliberate simplifications, does not pretend to offer one. If after reading it you feel that it has been helpful author and reader can feel satisfied. If it also stimulates your appetite for more, then we have both had a success.

Strategies
1. Models

Change has always been big business. Most societies have faced it in some form, whether political, military, social, economic or technological. How to make things happen, how to cope with change, live with it, love it and ultimately make use of it has fascinated humankind for millennia.

Despite its prevalence, however, enormous energy goes into resisting change. So what's new? Several factors are causing a rethink about how managers should handle change. First, there is the realization that organizational change is here to stay. We must stop opposing it and, like a judo expert, turn it to our advantage.

Chart 1
The goals managers seek

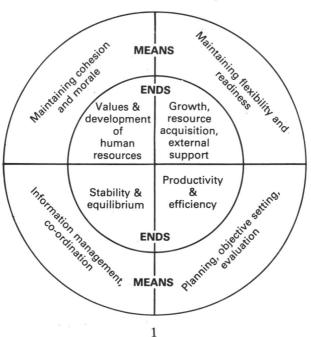

1

Stability was once a central management goal. The demand was for organizations in which you could predict and control events, organizations in which it was 'safe' to work. A manager worrying about stability becomes fixated on information and control. Harold Geneen, the legendary boss of ITT, epitomized this attitude. He had an astounding grasp of information. Nightly he left the office clutching several brief cases bulging with reports and accounts. Next day he returned, having read them all.

Yet stability is only one type of goal. Equally relevant are those shown in Chart 1. Organizations wanting to survive and grow must abandon the stifling effects of demanding certainty, predictability and minimal risk. Nor can they opt solely for growth, productivity or simply developing human assets.

Competing goals force us to accept that moving towards one may take us away from another. Hence we must be willing to accept a certain amount of instability. Taking this view to its logical conclusion the American efficiency specialist Tom Peters argues that 'success will come to those who love chaos – constant change, not those who attempt to eliminate it.'

Pace of change

The second factor that has forced a rethink in handling change is the accelerating pace of change. The impact has become so noticeable that in the 1970s Alvin Toffler dubbed it 'Future Shock' and people have been writing, researching and commenting on it ever since. What are these changes? They are varied and not easily

Box 1

Technological factors that will influence change
1   Genetic engineering
2   Electronic office
3   Automotive technology
4   Communications
5   Construction advances
6   Space technology
7   Energy
8   Military aerospace technology
9   Transportation
10 Medical technology
11 Robotics
12 New materials
13 Measurement tools
14 Personal computers and networks
15 Artificial intelligence

summarized except with rather unhelpful headings like political, social, demographic, economic forces.

If we analyse them in more detail, we begin to realize what is happening around us. Some of the technology factors are shown in Box 1. There are also complex social forces at work. Box 2 shows some 18 aspects of traditional life undergoing shifts likely to affect the environment in which organizations must exist. The dizzy pace of changes in company fortunes are more than enough to produce executive paranoia and stress. Only a few short years after quoting their examples of long term success stories, the authors of *In Search of Excellence* were explaining the adverse changes in fortunes of many of the original companies.

The changes that many organizations have had to face in a decade or so have been stunningly symbolized by the motor industry and its suppliers, but there are also plenty of examples in other fields, ranging from computers to mining, from local government to hotels. Today's manager knows that we are living in a period of rapid change, and today's business man does not need convincing of the necessity for responding to that change. As one European consultancy firm has pointed out:

> much that is written is like feeding horror stories to someone who is already living in a nightmare. It confirms his fears and strengthens his resolve to change but offers little practical help in the way of signposts or guidelines.

Many managers, unsure how to respond, become obsessed with structures, centralization versus decentralization, quality of work programmes, revamping incentive systems, new personnel systems and so on. Once it hardly mattered if change was approached in such a narrow way as there was scope to recover from any major mistakes. But for the foreseeable future the climate is turbulent and stressful, and the price of large scale failure has become unacceptably high.

Considering the mass of contradictory advice from often highly credible and respectable sources, it is no wonder that many managers believe that learning to handle change constructively only comes from hard won experience (see Box 3). Yet it is possible to make some sense of what seems to work. A useful starting point is to have a model of organizational change which you can personally use, a mind map which is not confined to text books and management courses.

There is no universal model or framework of organizational change, however, and each manager must arrive at their own by an amalgam of personal values, hunches, attitudes, beliefs and

Box 2

Emerging social changes

Traditional	Emerging
(1) Quality of life and quality of work life seen primarily in ' economic terms.	— Expanded quality of life and quality of working life values with growing emphasis on personal growth, self realisation, fit with social/physical environment.
(2) Long-term results orientation towards rewards (from savings, promotion, superannuation, rewards in heaven).	— Short-term rewards, hedonistic orientation – live now, buy now, pay later, enjoy immediate satisfaction.
(3) 'Protestant work ethic' – unquestioning acceptance of hard work, thrift – belief in free, capitalistic enterprise.	— Conditional work ethic depending on job security, interest challenge, growth opportunities – belief in controlled markets, cargo-cult, socialism.
(4) Accepted hierarchy of loyalties and responsibility – to God, country, family, class group.	— Variable loyalties and unclear responsibility; new hierarchy in descending order may be self, family, class group, country, God.
(5) Sanctity of property ownership, exploitative materialism, little concern for environment/ecology.	— Shift to rights of use and access to resources, awareness of societal ownership and ecological/environmental impacts.
(6) Relative community of interests among interdependent producer groups, along with rugged competitive individualism.	— Growing adversarial social group rivalries and competitions for special treatment, along with growing interdependence and collaboration within groups.
(7) Declining union membership among blue collar workers.	— Growing white collar and professional unionism.
(8) Acceptance of selected drugs (tobacco, alcohol).	— Acceptance of drug abuse as normal (hard drugs, drunkenness), decline in tobacco.
(9) Respect for authority of position and hierarchical decisions, trust in government.	— Growing disrespect for authority of position and government, growing respect for demonstrative expertise and desire for social consensus, participation in decision-making.
(10) Acceptance of the status quo, conformity to established social norms, stability and rountines.	— Acceptance of dissent, tolerance to non-conformity of social norms, innovations, change, flexibility.
(11) Acceptance of rigid moral and ethical principles of established religions.	— Relativism and more relaxed situation-based ethics and morals – gap between religious principles and practice.

(12) Acceptance of male dominance and double standards.	— Growing freedom of women, and toward economic, sexual, social equality.
(13) Racial cultural intolerance	— Greater acceptance of multi-racial, multi-cultural factors as enriching every society.
(14) Acceptance of paternalistic, but fair government and business, and of market mechanisms.	— Growing resentment and lack of trust, along with increasing demands on government and business.
(15) The individual as the basic unit and goal for social change – all men are equal.	— Social groups as the basic units which advance us as individuals – 'all men are equal but some are more equal than others'.
(16) Concern and resentment toward injustice (e.g. unemployment).	— Apathy, resignation, rationalization for injustice (eg unemployed are mainly dole bludgers), with the emergence of a semi-permanent class of jobless persons.
(17) A relatively even distribution of age cohorts in nuclear families.	— Rapidly ageing populations, with shift to non-nuclear families and isolation of oldies.
(18) Education mainly of young people, creating realistic expectancies.	— More education of young people and continuing education of adults, creating unrealistic expectations.

Source: 'Developing managers for social change', P Helius, *Journal of Management Development*, Vol 3, No 1, 1984

perceptions. Models are a mind set for thinking about something clearly. They stimulate more creative ways of tackling where, when and how to intervene to make things happen.

From here to there

The simplest framework for thinking about the change process appears in Chart 2 in which diagnosis of the need for change leads on to planning and eventually to interventions. The latter lead to more problems and opportunities producing a new round of diagnosis, planning and interventions. In various forms this model will be used throughout this book.

We can view change from several angles. The most personal is how we as individuals must change ourselves, adapt and cope. Another angle, of particular interest to managers, is how organizations as a whole change. Excessive usage has turned the phrase 'organizational change' into a woolly concept, but at its simplest it is about moving a situation in the organization from ·

HERE to ....,............................... THERE.

Box 3

Conflicting advice about change

Analyse the need for change thoroughly	Don't bother! Organizations are too complex to justify the effort
Don't rush into action. Be more reflective about the likely impact of change	Have a bias for action; beware of the paralysis of analysis; action precipitates change
We know little about the true levers of change	We know quite a lot! Research has uncovered the essential change process and how to make it happen
Resistance to change is bad	Resistance is functional and should be welcomed
When you have made a big change, evaluate before continuing	Maintain the momentum; heap change on change to get real results
Go to great lengths to tell people what changes you want	Avoid announcements; make changes quietly so they become established facts of life
Reactive management is bad	Reactive management is good
Managers should be highly pro-active	Managers are too prone to rush into action
Good managers do not need to use power relationships to achieve change	Effective managers use power relationships to foster change
Stability should follow from a major change effort	Stability is unattainable and undesirable
React to the environment to avoid organizational obsolescence	Act on the environment and transform it
Treat the organization as a giant system – everything depends on everything else	Treat the organization as merely loosely linked sub-systems
To manage change, manage the interdependencies	To manage change, promote individualism and personal autonomy
Change is best generated by good teamwork	Real change stems from rampant individualism and product or service champions
Go for evolutionary, step-by-step change	Go for radical transformations
Participation reduces the power gap between managers and sub-ordinates	Participation leaves the power gap unchanged, it merely links the needs of managers and sub-ordinates

Chart 2

A simplified view of the change process

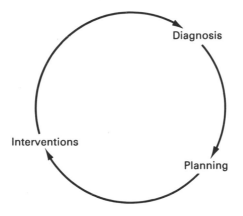

Change smashes the *status quo*, altering what happens in the enterprise. There are two main types of organizational change:

● Strategic

● Operational (day-to-day).

The first is highly distinctive and relates to the future direction of the organization affecting one or more of the goals shown in Chart 1. Strategic change involves some major switch in what the organization does and how it does it, and it usually takes place over months or years, rather than days or weeks.

Operational or day-to-day change, on the other hand, happens constantly. Managers are always either causing or responding to events which seldom in themselves amount to strategic change, although a succession of day-to-day events can accumulate into a significant shift. Another angle on operational change is that it is mainly opportunity change in which managers take advantage of situations to alter situations (see Chapter 8 on Planning).

The search for models

Missing from the mountainous pile of change literature, whether academic or autobiographical, are:

- A rigorously tested general model explaining how organizations work

- Levers of change, which are generally known to work (validated).

There have been numerous attempts at capturing the essence of organizations, most of it descriptive rather than explanatory and prescriptive. Efforts to nail down the precise nature of the change process have been considerable and from the shaky foundations has come endless and often dubious advice on what does or does not work.

A prescriptive general theory of organizational change would be of limited use in daily affairs. What works for multinational or global companies would probably be useless to the small business or a local district council. This lack of a tested model is frustrating for busy managers who want workable ideas and tools. It partly explains the phenomenal success of best selling management guides based on a limited series of case studies, or highly personal accounts such as Chrysler boss Lee Iacocca's views on how to manage change. His entertaining autobiography pushed his popularity to cult status and there was even talk of him standing for President. After the dust settles from such literary wisdom doubts surface about the usability of the advice and the hunger for new panaceas is renewed.

The sheer messiness of handling organizational change and the absence of validated models and theories are no reasons for ignoring what can sometimes be helpful ways of looking at the task of handling change to produce constructive results.

The changing models

Models and theories are tools for making sense of the change process and are often spurned because they:

- Do not accurately reflect the real world

- Are incomplete and can encourage narrow thinking

- Seldom offer detailed, validated guidance for action.

Despite these drawbacks they provide a rough framework, a mind set, within which to consider what results you want, how you might achieve them and the possible consequences of any actions. Apart from models of the change process itself there have been three important ways of viewing organizations that have influenced management thinking this century and hence how to achieve effective change: the traditional or classical model; the human relations model; and the systems model.

Traditional/classical model

The traditional/classical model sees organizations as machines, with layers of management, concerned mainly with mass production. Specialization is triumphant. What counts are the buzz words of scheduling, planning, organizing, monitoring, motivating, counselling and so on.

This model directs attention to spans of control and requires that people's authority matches their responsibilities. It has lost favour because it is rigid, predictable and does not reflect what actually occurs in real organizations.

Human relations model

Human relations models view organizations as living organisms with mutually connected and interdependent parts. Authority flows from below upwards, not from the top down. Groups have as much influence on change as the manager. This model is a reaction to the stark certainties of the mechanistic approach.

The buzz words for this model are managing groups, understanding the informal parts of the organization, an emphasis on democratic leadership, flat hierarchies and team development.

Systems model

The vagueness of the human relations model only served to remind managers that their organizations were complicated. The systems model is a response to growing size and complexity. Confusion is made manageable by treating the organization rather like a giant computer. Jargon from the computer field is used, such as inputs, outputs and various processes in between.

In a giant system everything is related to everything else. For managers the message is:

● To handle change well you must understand the whole, then unravel how the bits fit together.

The buzz words for this model are openness in relationships, need for rationality, team work and cohesive groups, interdependence, and so on. A version of this model is shown in Chart 3. The systems model has had a significant impact on how managers handle change, particularly advanced technology. It has focussed attention on what results the organization wants and is achieving.

Chart 3

A systems model

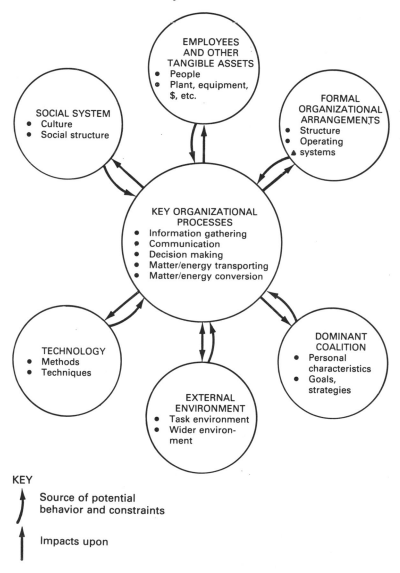

KEY

⌒ Source of potential
behavior and constraints

↑ Impacts upon

Source: J P Kotter, *Organizational Dynamics*, © 1978, Addison-Wesley Publishing
Company, Inc., Reading, Massachusetts. Reprinted with permission.

This model is losing its appeal because practical experience shows that mastering the interdependence of a giant, tightly linked system is beyond the skills of the majority of managers, no matter how well equipped they might be with analytical tools.

All three models have stimulated powerful suggestions for how managers should develop their organizations, such as Lickert's System 4 in which organizations move through various stages from authoritarian to participative; Blake's grid in which firms and managers move from concern only for production or only for people towards a more balanced approach; and McGregor's polarization of the management approach into authoritarian or participative with his Theory X and Theory Y.

The loosely-coupled system

From this battle ground of models has come a more pragmatic view of the organization. It is a realistic response to the extreme rate of change of our times.

Although the organization is still seen as various sub systems these are almost independent and only loosely linked to create the whole. They are systems of action rather than geographical chunks of the enterprise. The systems model makes managers take a macro look at the organization by expecting them to understand its parts by first understanding the whole. The loosely coupled model on the other hand asks managers to take a more micro view, expecting them to grasp the whole through understanding the parts.

This newer model accepts change and turbulence; despite their impact the entire system is bound together by shared values, sentiments and symbols. The manager is still concerned with inter-dependencies, but between different systems of action, not people. The main actor in this model is often the individual, not a group.

The buzz words for this model are decentralization, devolution, smaller corporate headquarters, smaller business units, and the autonomy of individuals. A version of this model is shown in Chart 4.

For senior managers interested in handling change the loosely coupled model has important implications. One of the main tasks of top management is managing the organization's culture and values. Managers are concerned with developing an overall vision with which to inspire and direct the sub systems (see Chapter 3 on Vision and Values).

Teamwork is taken for granted. Individuals are not trapped by the group's boundaries. When the interests of the organization demand it individuals act to transform and if necessary transcend the group. In this model the personal values which individual

Chart 4

The renewal ring

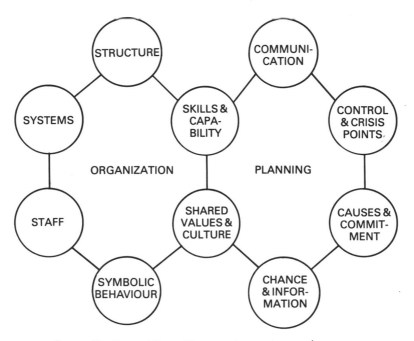

Source: *The Renewal Factor*, Waterman J. Jn, Bantam Press, 1988

employees hold are important, not a minor irritation. What counts is how you promote the freedom of the individual to work with others for the benefit of the organization. Thus personal autonomy has a central place in this particular model.

Strengthening the individual's role is a particular challenge for managers. It has been seen to work, for example, in abolishing quality inspectors and putting the responsibility where it belongs, with those actually doing the work. Widening the individual's role means tolerating ambiguity, independence, and an ability to deal with complexity. Consequently the management skills for handling change are different to those previously expected (see Chart 5). There is more emphasis on empathy and feelings, on transforming skills such as visualization techniques and on certain types of mental abilities such as seeing the 'big picture' (see also Chapter 2 on Leadership).

Loosely coupled sub systems are an alternative to seeing change

Chart 5

New skills managers need for handling change

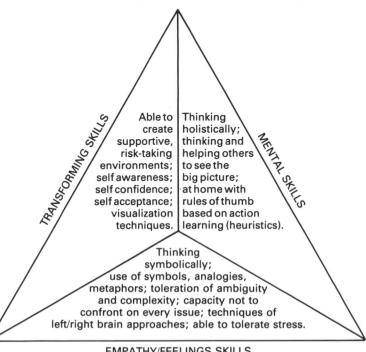

as occurring in a giant system which the manager must somehow learn to master. Instead, change is a developmental process in which **growth** and **direction** are the main issues – the model is going somewhere. Everyone is a change agent. The manager can be seen less as an analyst and more like a gardener tending a plant, watching and helping it grow in its own natural direction.

Using this model enables you to identify expectations about the future, both your own and the organization's. 'Where are we going?' becomes a central issue along with 'how are we going to get there?'

Relevance

Perhaps you feel that viewing your organization in this way is irrelevant and unrelated to practical use? Are you so sure? The revitalized role of the individual for example, can already be seen in job advertisements for those with leadership skills, in the major thrust by both the public and private sector to decentralize, eliminate large headquarters, in the search for product and service innovators and in the style of training that increasingly stresses concepts from this new model.

In Britain's public sector it can be seen for instance in the contracting out of certain services and the emergence of new relationships between various groups, as between:

- The council and central government departments

- The council and private tenderers

- The council and grant receiving bodies

- Managers and subordinates

- Managers and professionals

- Professionals and those in receipt of their services

- One department and another.

In the loosely coupled model managers achieve change by influencing the sub systems, not the entire enterprise in one go. Since there are many sub systems it can be helpful to reduce these to manageable proportions as in the strategic rope (Chart 6) in which the organization is simplified into three woven-together strands: technical, cultural, political.

As with a rope these strands are not easily distinguished from a distance. In achieving strategic change the management role is to unravel the strands and then work on one or more in depth; secondly to knit them together again so that change is implemented and made permanent. Integrating the strands is an ongoing management activity, not a once only event.

The strategic rope idea is also useful because it draws attention to a common tendency amongst practising managers to put their trust in a single way of achieving change. Regardless of the nature of the problem some managers will always restructure, others will always improve communications, whilst others will always alter how services or goods are produced.

To affect the three sub systems managers can use the tools of mission or strategy, structure, administrative and human resource

Chart 6

Strands of the strategic rope

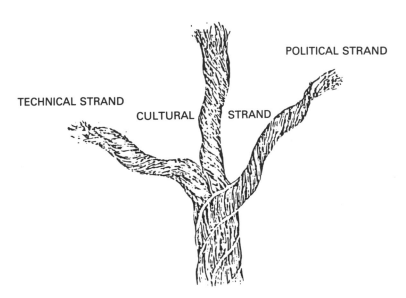

Chart 7

Strategic change model

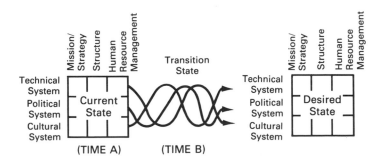

Source (of both charts): 'Essentials of strategic management', by Noel Tichey, *Journal of Business Strategy* (USA), Spring 1983

procedures. Chart 7 shows Noel Tichey's strategic change model. It emphasizes time, the movement from

HERE to .... THERE.

In changing from one state to another the organization passes through a separate transition phase. Whether it takes a long or short time to complete this phase the transition phase is distinctly different from the desired or end state.

This picture of change focusses our attention on a usually much neglected issue, namely 'what happens before we reach the end state?' Managing the transition state can be a complex task requiring considerable skill. Some managers are much better at initiating change and handling the transition stage than they are the results of the transformation. Some people prefer developing and creating while others enjoy consolidating and systematizing.

GUIDELINES

- DISTINGUISH between strategic and operational change

- DEVELOP a personal model of organizational change which you find helpful – not one confined to the text books and management courses.

- USE models to help stimulate and clarify thinking about change and the consequences

- AVOID putting trust in one way of achieving change. Use the strategic rope concept of technical, cultural, political strands to consider how to tackle change.

- GIVE attention to the transition stage of change not merely the end state.

Strategies
2. Leadership

Jack Goodwin spent most of his life making gear boxes. He helped make Rolls Royces and assumed that the only time he would get to ride in one was 'when I'd be in a wooden box'. Then in 1984 the Crewe based company started a scheme whereby all its 3,800 employees were invited to ride once in the cars which they had spent their working lives making.

So Jack Goodwin had his ride in the Rolls Royce Silver Spur, along with men who had been making its upholstery for 30 years. Men like Jack, who began assembling gear boxes during the Korean war, spent their once in a lifetime ride straining their ears to detect a gear change.

It is easy to dismiss the Rolls decision to have all its employees drive in one of the world's most luxurious cars as cynical, a sop to industrial democracy. As the Quality Improvement Manager put it:

> At first a lot of people thought it was a gimmick – 'What are they after now?' sort of thing. Some said they weren't bothered, but it was quite different afterwards. I mean, you see the cars made, but you're making bits and pieces. It isn't until you ride in one that you see what it's all about.

Seeing what it is all about, beginning to really care about one's work, is a sign that management leadership is being effective.

What is leadership?

The simplest view of leadership is that it helps turn plans and decisions into action. Leadership is when:

> people with certain motives and purposes mobilize resources so as to arouse, engage and satisfy the motives of followers.

This view reflects two principal leadership styles. The first is when leaders give followers what they want in exchange for things sought

17

by the leader. The two parties may be seeking different results, and the relationship is thus transactional. The second leadership style is when leaders create situations in which the ends are desired by both leaders and followers. In this case the leaders raise the sights and aspirations of followers, and the relationship is thus a transforming one.

Virtually every research finding about leadership has been challenged or contradicted by other studies. Leadership is a sophisticated concept with as many different definitions as people who have attempted to define it (see Box 4).

Box 4

Different ways of looking at leadership

- A focus of group processes
- Personality and its effects
- The art of inducing compliance
- An exercise in influence
- Act or behaviour
- A form of persuasion
- Power relationship
- An instrument of goal achievement
- A way of defining an individual's role

The importance of leadership in achieving change stretches back to man's early history. It is therefore tempting to think that good leaders are born with, rather than create, the required qualities. Within organizations what has altered in recent years is first the realization that leadership is not the exclusive preserve of the most senior manager, and secondly that today's leaders who make things happen are transformational, they revitalize entire organizations.

Everybody does it

Anybody can play a leadership role, depending on the local situation. During a major change effort, leadership may move around the organization and be shared by many different people. In fact situations throw up leaders and leadership skills can certainly be learned both through work experience as well as carefully targeted training.

In 1985 United Technologies, a major US aerospace company which has diversified into a multinational concern, began trying to define what it meant by leadership. It gradually narrowed the field to:

- A clear sense of direction

- An ability to involve the whole organization in clarifying that direction

- A willingness to encourage initiative and risk taking – and tolerance of failure

- A management style that empowers people to do the job without abdicating accountability

- An emphasis on teamwork.

To help all its managers achieve these objectives UT managers concluded that they needed to practise a range of skills including: creating and developing a shared vision; taking initiatives; empowering others; and gaining support in the organization. The UT view of leadership stems from a highly practical need to turn a much misused concept into a management tool.

Transformational leadership reflects the realization that most Western commercial organizations need to fundamentally rethink how they operate in order to survive in the face of fierce, at times brutal, competitive pressures. Public bodies too are facing similar demands for radical change. A local authority, for instance, asked to cut its spending by as much as 20 per cent is no longer in the cosy business of turning the wheels of the bureaucratic machine.

Transforming is a three act drama of recognizing the need for revitalization, creating a new vision and institutionalizing changes. This is an endless cycle as shown in Chart 8.

The leadership tasks

From a combination of research and the practical experience of companies such as United Technologies, we have a rough idea about what managerial leaders do to make things happen. These are shown in Box 5.

A clear sense of direction
Abraham Lincoln's administration was once criticized for stumbling along. The president's reply was that while this might be true

Chart 8

Transformational leadership: a three-act drama

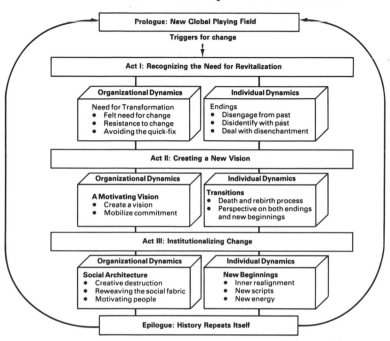

Source: *The Transformational Leader*, Tichey N, Devanra M, John Wiley, 1986

'we are stumbling in the right direction'. A sense of direction, knowing 'where we are going' is what makes leaders attractive to followers. While managers often become stuck in a morass of objectives, leaders are more concerned with a general direction than detailed targets.

Similarly managers are usually concerned with balancing operations in an organization, relating to others according to their role. They are detached, impersonal, seek solutions acceptable as a compromise among conflicting values and identify totally with the organization. By contrast managerial leaders focus on direction and matters of principle.

Leaders create new approaches and imagine new areas to explore. They relate to people more intuitively and in empathetic ways, moving to where opportunity and reward are high, and projecting ideas into images which excite people. Since the road to

Box 5

How managers offer leadership

- **A clear sense of direction** (objectives)
  - define goals
  - involve whole organization in clarifying that direction
  - provide means for goal attainment
  - maintain goal direction

- **Values**
  - engender core values
  - pursue core values with total persistence and meticulous attention to details which help achieve this end
  - constant interaction with employees to promote core values

- **Excitement**
  - engender this amongst employees

- **Teamwork**
  - emphasis on teamwork
  - provide and maintain group structure
  - facilitate group interactions
  - maintain member satisfaction
  - facilitate group task performance

- **Accountability**
  - empower people to do the job without abdicating accountability
  - encourage initiative and risk taking
  - tolerate failure

---

the final goal may be a long one, leaders also have the task of helping people to keep their sights on the end results and not become diverted to less relevant ones. They must be able to see and hold onto 'the big picture' (see also below).

Values

While it is possible that leadership and management may coincide, it is nevertheless true that effective managers are not always good leaders and successful leaders may sometimes be poor managers. What seems to set leaders apart from managers is found in the idea which the Woolworths UK management adopted in their work of changing their organization:

- Managers do it right, leaders do what is right.

The car rides for all employees at Rolls Royce were not just propaganda. They were also an exercise in leadership to highlight and enhance core values. Like children able to see beyond a play-ground for the first time, the upholsterers, for example, began marvelling at the engineering and the engineers at the comfort. 'It's beautiful, beautiful,' commented one upholstery fitter who did not even own a car.

Effective leadership pays meticulous attention to details that engender and show in practical ways the importance of core values. For example, a clothes manufacturer who declares that 'quality comes first' does little by his words to actually promote this value; removing every faulty item and asking all employees to attend a ritual burning of the defective goods would make the point more forcibly.

In 1986 managers at ICL's high technology Kidsgrove plant introduced a zero defect policy which meant that no single part of the operation was allowed to pass on doubtful work to another. Though plant productivity fell, customer satisfaction soared. A series of courses was mounted to help managers cope with change, leading to a realization that there had to be high quality communi-cations. As the manager of the Process Production centre put it:

> we were not only reconciled to losing our total work force
> for half an hour per week for briefing sessions but we could
> see the positive results of total involvement in the business . . .

Leadership persistence in pursuing core values demands that these become a high priority for everyone. For example, the Adult Services Division of the London Borough of Croydon identified a core value as 'improving the quality of our services by actively involving users and their relatives'. To translate this statement into action senior management asked every team in the division to identify ways of doing this as part of setting their own annual objectives. Thus virtually all members of the staff were involved in discussing and planning the pursuit of the core value of involving users. It was further backed up with training support on how to be more helpful to users and their relatives.

Effective management leadership seeks to ensure a constant interaction with employees to promote core values. This goes beyond sending round notices or putting up posters. Management must be out and about communicating or modelling the importance of core values and hearing what obstacles there are to turning these values into a reality (see also Chapter 3 on Vision and Values).

Excitement
Change through leadership also means causing excitement, as the Rolls Royce example above shows. Some years ago a leading

computer company booked a football stadium to announce and praise the successes of its sales force. The huge electronic score board flashed up the sales results of each individual salesman as they came running onto the pitch to cheers from the audience of employees, friends and relatives. Outrageous? Perhaps, yet employees of the company still talk about it to this day. Excitement keeps alive those values and goals that leaders want to pursue.

Teamwork
Most managers will affirm that they believe in teamwork; leaders actually achieve it. Sometimes this is done with team building skills. Occasionally, however, using teams stems from fear – people are forced to use teams as a defensive way of coping with anxiety or uncertainty. Effective leaders must model good behaviour by paying attention to team work in their own working group of senior managers (see Chapter 19 on Team Building).

Accountability
Interest has been growing in recent years in how organizations can promote the employees' autonomy. This concern reflects the extent to which leadership has previously been relegated to a back seat in favour of the managerial role.

In managing change leaders hand over power in numerous ways. They accept that goals can only be achieved if people accept responsibility for taking initiatives. How far this approach permeates throughout the organization depends on management style. A participating style, such as that adopted in United Technologies, will expect this accountability to go both wide and deep.

Leaders also refuse to become embroiled in areas of responsibility which rightly belong to their subordinates. By constantly asking 'why can't you deal with it?' leaders challenge their followers to assert themselves and maximize their own use of authority and accountability.

Leadership skills

Learning the various activities associated with the leadership of change does not depend solely on an inherited talent. It may often rely on being thoroughly tenacious about finding new ways to undertake key tasks.

Increasingly organizations are operating as groups of sub systems which are loosely connected, not as single systems in which managers must understand all the complicated interdependencies. In this loosely coupled system leadership demands rather different skills to those associated with more traditional models of the organization (see Chapter 1 on Models).

If organizations are just a bunch of loosely linked sub systems whose connections are hard to understand, managers need leadership skills if they are to manage change adequately. These skills include:

- Transforming

- Ability to get things done

- Ability to see the big picture

- Ability to think clearly

- Personal maturity.

Transforming skills
Across the industrial and commercial landscape we are seeing the emergence of a new breed of leader – the transformational leader. These people take on the responsibility for revitalizing an organization, defining the need for change, creating new visions and mobilizing commitment to these visions. Ultimately they intend to transform the organization. This kind of thinking demands new thinking about strategy, structure and people.

The ability to manage and relate to people is now widely seen as a core skill in managing change. There is a stress on combining right brained activity (thinking which is creative and intuitive) with left brained thinking (that which is systematic, logical and rational).

In tomorrow's organizations the recognition of the autonomy of the individual will have a central place in management thinking and action. Already there are clear signs that advanced organizations are recognizing this in highly practical ways.

One of the most publicized developments, pioneered by the Xerox Corporation, has been the idea of networking, in which employees are encouraged to leave the payroll to establish their own organization which directly serves the mother firm which guarantees a certain amount of paid work on regular contract. Transforming leadership is thus able to find ways to develop and supervise autonomous individuals rather than depend on exercising coercive or hierarchical power in the more traditional way.

Managers will have to develop such skills increasingly if they want to produce results. In practical terms it means that you as a manager may have to:

- DEPEND less on your position in the hierarchy and more on your expertise, leadership and personality

- PAY more attention to what a wider range of other people in the organization think and say

- ADAPT easily to new information and situations

- ATTEND more to your own and other people's intuition

- PLACE more value on the creative, experimenting style of making things happen

- RELY less on rules, systems, procedures and control and hence live with a greater degree of risk and uncertainty

- RECOGNIZE the needs of followers to satisfy their higher needs of personal development, autonomy and self realization.

Ability to get things done

Making things happen is what managing change is all about. Where the various sub systems are often only connected by fairly tenuous links, effective leadership of change stresses proactive, transforming skills. The individual manager is motivated by an inner drive. Peters and Waterman's study of *Excellence* showed that a bias for action was a common feature of successful companies.

To get things done requires a manager to be more than responsive to people and situations. It demands pragmatic common sense combined with a good knowledge of the organization's principal aims. In practical terms it means that you as a manager may have to:

- FORMULATE your own goals

- EVALUATE your own successes and failures with ruthless and sometimes painful honesty

- SEEK constantly to clarify and simplify aims so that the tasks to make them happen are clearly identified and allocated

- GO beyond your own job boundaries and take an interest in events throughout the whole organization

- TEST constantly whether proposed action is really achievable and desirable

- KEEP an eye on the 'bottom line' which may be profitability, quality of service, morale and so on.

Ability to see the big picture

Organizational change means influencing the technical, cultural and political elements of the enterprise (see opening chapter). In the process it is easy to lose sight of the overall picture of what is being attempted. Managers constantly have to resist becoming bogged down in activities which, on reflection, are not really central to core values and priority tasks.

Wisse Dekker who in 1982 was appointed president and chairman of the giant Philips company, based in Eindhoven, Holland, was able to see the wood for the trees when despite the enormous complexity of the multinational concern he concluded:

> my first priority was to communicate a sense of urgency to our employees. I had to make clear to our generally comfortable staff that Philips could not continue to survive without dramatic changes.

Thus leadership of change requires managers to avoid becoming trapped in side issues, details, paper work or irrelevancies. In practical terms it means that you as a manager may have to:

- DEVELOP political and networking skills in which you learn to read the political and economic climate

- LOOK outward beyond your own work area and the organization itself

- ACQUIRE public relations skills, in particular learning how to handle the media

- ORGANIZE how you spend your time and limited energy

- MAXIMIZE delegation

- BUILD yourself good channels of communication and systems for monitoring what is happening.

Ability to think clearly

It is no coincidence that in the last few years there has been a rush of books and publications and training courses offering to help managers think more clearly and creatively about their work. The quality of your leadership depends on the quality of your thinking.

In organizations which are constructed of separate sub systems with links of varying strengths, managers must be extremely clear about goals and responsibilities, and be able to think through what they are trying to achieve. Intuition, right brain activity and the concept of thinking laterally, all form part of the culture of change. There is less emphasis on managers mastering their environment and more on being able to ask 'what if?' questions.

Hence the leadership task is to demand information about likely outcomes, not simply to say 'this is what we are going to do', though of course it still considers assessments of risk and coping with uncertainty. In practical terms it means that you as a manager may have to:

- FOCUS attention on defining clear aims

- SEARCH constantly for new ways of doing things

- TAKE few plans or proposals for granted

- DEVELOP scenarios of possible outcomes and evaluate these systematically.

Personal maturity
Maturity can be defined as how far a person is willing and able to take responsibility for their own behaviour. The effectiveness of your leadership of the change effort will depend on two aspects of maturity: your own and that of your followers.

Follower maturity
Researchers Hersey and Blanchard have argued that maturity should only be considered in relation to a specific task. You cannot generalize and say an employee is 'mature or immature'. People bring different degrees of maturity to the tasks which they perform. Though age brings maturity in one sense, it does not guarantee that a person develops a mature personality.

An important conclusion from this view of maturity is that there is no one best way to influence people. The leadership style that you should adopt with an individual or group depends on their maturity. Management leadership behaviour can be classified into:

- DIRECTION or task behaviour
  How much direction you provide, for example telling people what to do, how to do it and when. In a small group, for instance, the tasks include: initiating; elaborating or clarifying; co-ordinating; summarizing; and recording.

- SUPPORT or relationship behaviour
  The extent of a two-way communication with your people, including active listening; offering supportive and facilitating behaviour. In a small group this would include encouraging; reducing tension; and gate keeping.

A combination of task behaviour and relationship behaviour produces four specific leadership styles: telling, selling, participating and delegating.

In exercising leadership you choose an appropriate style which reflects your followers' level of maturity. The maturity of followers can be graded along a continuum. Thus, selecting an appropriate leadership style depends on the right combination of direction and support in relationship to the maturity of followers. To diagnose the style required you can use the curve shown in Chart 9.

Telling is appropriate for low maturity followers, selling should be used with followers who have a low to moderate maturity and participating is suitable for moderate to high maturity. Delegating is reserved for followers of high maturity. This approach, called Situational Leadership suggests that to offer leadership of the change effort you must:

- ASSESS the maturity level of those you want to influence

- CONSIDER ways to help followers grow in their maturity as far as they are willing and able

- ADJUST your own behaviour appropriately.

Your maturity
Situational Leadership demands that managers develop a good insight into their own behaviour and thinking. First, because to make things happen you require the active, committed help of other people. By knowing your own strengths and weaknesses you can more easily decide what type of help you need.

Secondly, leading a major change effort is a demanding role, usually involving considerable interaction with other people. This too is made easier and more effective if you have insight into how you perform during such interactions.

Thirdly, self awareness enables you to respond better during change. If you know that you tend to avoid risk taking, have a tendency to procrastinate or demand too much information before making a decision, then you can find ways to deal with these traits.

Chart 9

Leadership styles

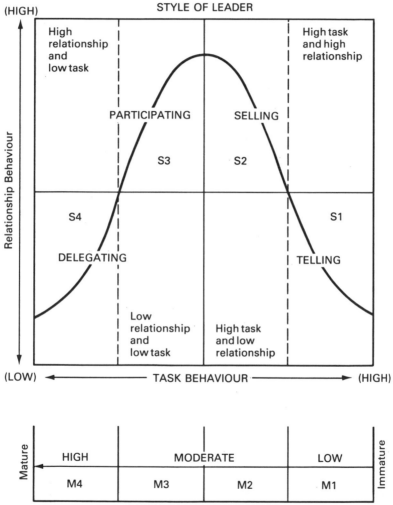

(HIGH)   STYLE OF LEADER

High relationship and low task

High task and high relationship

PARTICIPATING   SELLING

S3   S2

S4   S1

DELEGATING   TELLING

Low relationship and low task

High task and low relationship

Relationship Behaviour

(LOW) ◄——— TASK BEHAVIOUR ———► (HIGH)

	Mature				Immature	
	HIGH		MODERATE		LOW	
	M4	M3	M2	M1		

MATURITY OF FOLLOWER(S)

Continuous self evaluation is therefore a common feature of effective leaders of major change efforts. They are always mentally reviewing their own performance, seeking new ways to be more effective.

An aspect of maturity which is not tied to chronological age is the ability to cope with stress. Sometimes younger managers are better able to handle stresses than their older colleagues who may see too many angles on a situation or become over-committed to certain people, ideas or ways of working which are being challenged by the change effort. A leader who handles stress well is likely to be more effective than one who does not (see also Chapter 12 on Stress).

A mature personality in practical terms means that you as a manager may have to:

- SPEND time regularly assessing your own strengths and weaknesses

- SEEK help willingly to review your personal performance objectively

- CREATE a personal development programme, either within your organization or outside it

- ACQUIRE a strong commitment to, or acceptance of, the values of the organization; develop loyalty

- LEARN how to handle stress well.

The sign of a mature personality is that the manager copes well in a turbulent environment. Things get done despite both real and psychological barriers to change. The manager learns to live with and help others cope with complexity, uncertainty and ambiguity.

Finally, what do the successful leaders in organizations tend to be like? Box 6 shows the sort of qualities such people are likely to possess.

Box 6

Qualities of successful organizational leaders

- INTELLIGENCE – slightly higher than the average of their followers with an ability to analyse, comprehend situations and communicate effectively

- BREADTH AND MATURITY – generally possess broader interests than their followers; more shock proof, more mature emotionally and not over-elated by success or crushed by failure

- MOTIVATION AND DRIVE FOR ACHIEVEMENT – a strong personal need to keep achieving something; constantly seeking self realization and creativity and work hard for satisfaction of inner drives rather than material rewards

- ATTITUDE TO PEOPLE – understand that they can only get their job done through others; develop a healthy respect for people and a skill in relating to them; employee orientated, approach problems in terms of people rather than technical aspects

- SPECIALIST KNOWLEDGE AND SKILLS – tend to have greater specialist knowledge and skill than followers in the particular specialization of the group

---

GUIDELINES

- CREATE and protect core values

- PERSIST in pursuing core values

- SEEK constant interaction with employees to promote core values

- ENGENDER excitement

- RELY less on your position in the hierarchy and more on your expertise, leadership and personality

- LISTEN to what a wide range of other people in the organization think and say

- RESPOND willingly to new information and situations

- VALUE your own and other people's intuition

- SUPPORT the creative, experimenting style of making things happen

- DEPEND less on rules, systems, and procedures and more on creativity, flair and a sense of direction

- EVALUATE constantly your own successes and failures

- LOOK beyond your own job boundaries; take an interest in events throughout the organization

- TEST constantly whether proposed action is really achievable and desirable

- DEVELOP public relations skills, in particular learning how to handle the media

- ORGANIZE how you spend your time and limited energy

- MAXIMIZE delegation

- BUILD good channels of communication and systems for monitoring what is happening

- SEEK new ways of doing things

- TAKE few plans or proposals for granted

- CREATE scenarios of possible outcomes and evaluate these systematically

- ASSESS the maturity level of those you want to influence

- HELP followers grow in their maturity as far as they are willing and able

- DEVISE a personal development programme, either within your organization or outside it

- LEARN to handle stress well.

Strategies
3. Vision and values

The chimney stood tall and bleak against the grey landscape. The last explosive charges had been inserted, checks completed on all the connections. The demolition expert threw a switch and with a roar 250 foot of brick and cement collapsed into a mountain of rubble.

When he pulled the switch the demolition expert had a clear mental picture of the final result he was expecting. Nothing less than the entire chimney had to crumble, no part of the structure should be left standing. Success was a pile of old bricks.

Managers wanting to achieve successful change also need a strong mental image of the result. A vision of the end results sounds mystical. For simple day-to-day changes it merely means being able to communicate a clear idea about the result so that other people can share in and identify with your picture of the future. It must be realistic enough for other people to see themselves and their part in it.

For major organizational change vision demands more than a simple mind picture of the end result. It means starting with a guiding philosophy that grabs people's attention and excites them. This need not be expressed in complicated or metaphysical ways. For example, Woolworths' Chief Executive Geoffrey Mulcahy explained to his shareholders that what drove him and his colleagues forward was the determination to become 'the most profitable retail stores group in the country'.

Creating a vision nails our colours to the mast. We state what the preferred future would look like. Vision channels our deepest values into the work place, it is a word picture of how we see our values working. What makes organizations tick is not products, strategies or technology, it is people who are motivated by ideas, hopes and aspirations. These must be graspable by everyone – the vision must be easily shared. Managers become less concerned with manipulating things and people and more with manipulating ideas and concepts.

Vision does not replace the need for rational, analytical methods such as budgeting, reporting, control systems, objective setting

33

and other quantitative measures. These are all necessary for running organizations. They are, however, capable of stifling innovation, creativity and the ability to drop existing plans and develop entirely new directions and achievements.

Vision is closely connected to leadership which supplies and translates it into ways of making it a reality. In the depths of the crisis at Apple Computer in 1984 and 1985, for example, when the survival of the company was in doubt, President John Sculley wrestled with keeping the firm afloat by taking practical steps such as cutting inventories, restructuring and axing a complete factory. He also found time to agonize over the vision for the future of the company. He met many of the industry's pioneers who helped him define the company's new vision; he devoured books showing how non technologists like himself could be as passionate and visionary as the industry's pioneer inventors. 'I had to go on a search, to track the dream back to its source'.

These days most managers have heard about vision and vision building and there is a danger that it will soon be relegated to the list of management techniques 'we tried and which did not work'. Perhaps more than any other aspect of achieving change, vision demands persistence and single-mindedness which must withstand sometimes outrageous pressures and temptations. The call for compromise, to abandon principles, to go for the easy fix are like the siren voices which Ulysses blocked out with wax in the ears. Equally the ability to modify the vision, altering it to fit new opportunities, is also important in keeping it alive.

Making it happen

Setting the vision apart from all the other words and documents jostling for attention is that it:

● Expresses ideals

● Inspires

● Provides core values – against which plans, actions, and decisions can be judged

● Does not define exactly how the end result will be achieved

● Is understandable by absolutely everyone

● Is what top management live by.

Vision is therefore a sincere expression of what we want. Unlike goals or objectives it is not precise. It is a licence to dare, to be better despite inertia and blockages. It mobilizes people around what is not yet experienced.

In contrast to a mission statement, which says what kind of business we are in or compares our ranking against competitors, vision aims to capture our imagination and 'turn us on'. It will not contain numbers, complicated words, too many sentences, or be forgettable.

- Vision is about VALUES – or what really matters

- Mission is about PURPOSE – or what business we are in

- Objectives are about STRATEGY – or how we will get there.

How do visions work? They make explicit what people want to do anyway, which is why they are so closely tied to good leadership. Leaders articulate what followers want, then show how to make it happen. Through visions managers who are leaders influence an organization's norms which decide how change will be received and managed. Norms are hidden values which are in the areas shown in Box 7.

Vision affects change when the values which it represents start permeating people's daily behaviour. That is why vision has to be lofty, and try to inspire. If people do not feel inwardly drawn to it vision will make no impact, regardless of exhortation, monitoring or training.

Box 7

Where norms – the hidden values – are found

- Organizational and personal pride
- Performance and excellence
- Teamwork and communication
- Leadership and supervision
- Profitability and cost effectiveness
- Colleague relationships
- Customer and consumer relations
- Honesty and security
- Training and development
- Innovation and change

Building a vision statement

There are not 20 easy ways to build a vision. Creating one is a personal experience even if that occurs within a group. Because vision comes from within, developing it is a creative act. If you are going to live by a creed it cannot be produced by the marketing department or a committee of 'experts'. A vision statement is usually written down and built from core values such as those shown in Box 8.

Box 8

Some core values that may guide the vision

- We care about keeping our customers satisfied
- Everyone has the right to disagree
- We listen to what customers say
- We accept that success means tolerating failures
- What we say we will mean
- Being a manager is about supporting one's staff
- We believe in initiative and risk taking
- Quality comes first
- Value each employee as an individual

It takes time to identify these values. It is important to avoid producing slick slogans that have no gut feel and in which no one apart from the top management can really believe. You will know when you have anything approaching a vision statement if you and lots of other people agree that what it represents goes beyond an aim and should become a crusade. Crusades require zealots.

Developing a vision is messy, it evolves from past experience, making lists, talking with other people, encouraging people to participate in the task, chatting about what matters, what brought you into this line of work, scribbling on flip charts, asking what people think. If you do this and identify some core values you may eventually be able to convert them into a statement which spells out the vision.

Values exercise

Since values underpin the vision you may find it helpful to conduct a values exercise with colleagues. There is nothing particularly demanding in organizing this exercise and it does not need a consultant or trainer to do it. It is fun and can be both revealing and stimulating. The purpose is to discover how far you all share the same set of values and, if so, whether these can then be refined into a vision statement. To conduct the values exercise you need the items shown in Box 9.

The session starts with you or the senior manager responsible for the work group explaining about the importance of vision and values. Alternatively, give everyone a copy of the material below, down to the start of the description of the values exercise.

Box 9

Tools for a values exercise

Flip chart paper

One or more sets of 20–30 stiff cards measuring 3″ by 8″ on which are written core values (see below)

Blu-Tack and felt marker pens

One or more quiet rooms, preferably away from the normal work place

Some core values for use in the exercise

Accountable	Planned
Achieving	Profit driven
Action minded	Quality first
Adaptable	Respectful
Approachable	Responsible
Caring	Responsive
Close to the customer	Rewarding
Competitive	Risk taking
Excellence	Safe
Experimental	Sharing
Fair	Trusting
Friendly	Truthful
Fun	Useful
Innovative	Value for money
Leading	Valuing people
Original	
Open	

Add and substitute your own ideas that reflect your organization's thinking.
TIME: Allow at least two or three hours to complete the task.

The group now discusses what seems to be really important about the organization in which they currently work. What really matters, justifies its existence and makes it worth working for? Spend around 20 minutes doing this. It is a warming up which helps people think about values.

Hand out the Values Cards along with some Blu-Tack. The list of values given in Box 9 are only examples. Prepare a set which is considered relevant to your organization. For instance, a local council will not usually include profit making as a core value. Likewise a high risk venture capital company will probably not have safety as a core value. There should be at least 20–30 cards. If you are unsure as to what values should be written on the cards make this a first exercise for you and your colleagues. Ask them to identify some core values which either are or should be what the organization is all about.

Once you have a set of cards divide them out to the group. If there are more than five or six people divide them into smaller syndicates, giving them each a set of the Values Cards. After the Values Cards have been distributed you explain that the task is to select only five core values which the group as a whole feels most represents the vision or philosophy which should underpin the whole organization.

These five should be put in rank order; the most important value being number one, the next most important number two and so on. To make the selection the group can stick the cards on the walls and keep rearranging them until it arrives at the final selection. Allow about 40 minutes for this work to be done.

Because there are so many values from which to choose, many of which seem important, people have to think and debate hard about which ones matter and which are less important. The task is often difficult and the resulting discussions and 'arguments can be challenging and enlightening. When the five values have been chosen the group spends up to 20 minutes discussing these, why they have emerged and what they mean.

The final task is to convert the five values into a single visionary statement reflecting the kind of organization in which people feel they should be working.

Although this exercise may produce a vision statement it will probably not be the definitive one. It may take weeks or months to develop a truly compelling one which excites people.

In a division of the London Borough of Croydon Social Services department providing services to adults, for example, the following core values were identified:

- A planned, quality service

- Responsive to users

- The independence, normality, dignity and self respect of service recipients

- Improving and maintaining services

- Involving users and relatives.

These were combined into a statement of the division's basic philosophy:

> We work in a planned and responsive way with the users of our service to ensure that they can live as independently as possible with dignity and self respect. The quality of our service will be improved and maintained by actively involving users and their relatives.

Similarly, Levi Strauss, the jeans and clothes maker has a vision statement which begins that it should be 'a great company' and reflect a commitment to:

> . . . excellence in everything we do and with all its constituents. We will achieve greatness through a commitment to the following goals and practices . . .

The goals and practices are then listed under headings such as People; Customers; Retail Stores; and Suppliers.

Plenty of organizations have a vision statement, though they may not always call it that. Having articulated such a vision many organizations then breath a sigh of relief and get on with doing what they have always done in the past. A vision only becomes a force for change when it converts inspiration into action by:

- Communication – the vision is shared to gain support

- Persistence – a consistency of focus, keeping moving in the right direction even when the going gets tough

- Use of power – harnessing the energies and abilities of others to bring about real change

- Monitoring – discovering how we are doing compared to what we want to achieve

- Rearranging – altering how resources, including people, are used.

Because vision sounds mystical or metaphysical managers are sometimes reluctant to talk of 'vision' or even communicate their own view of the future in case they are thought unrealistic. The successful management of change demands that managerial leaders make others aware of the vision of the future and keep them focussed on it. You have to become comfortable talking about the future in ways which command people's attention.

Though you may have doubts about how to reach the vision, there is a need to communicate hope and optimism. To sound convinced in order to be persuasive you need to be willing and able to occasionally use emotionally charged words and phrases that catch and hold people's attention. If you talk that way so will other people. Be prepared to use words which bring colour and excitement to the language. Words like success, excellence, caring, service, are not out of place. Being a good manager does not mean always appearing down to earth, highly practical and pragmatic.

In conveying their vision of both the present and the future, managerial leaders use metaphors, word pictures, imagery, parables and examples. Uncomplicated explanations or diagrams get ideas across. A company director, for instance, wanting to persuade colleagues to invest in making a new project more imaginative than originally planned explained: 'it's like the difference between black and white television and colour. Although you can do without colour, you'll much prefer it'. When, for instance, Roy Griffiths, Manager and Chairman of the Sainsbury Stores and adviser to the government on health and community services, reported how these might be changed he used vivid word pictures such as:

> . . . it is not the road blocks to achievement which are the major problems, but the vehicles themselves.

> There is no neat solution waiting to be discovered – no Rubik Cube which will be perfectly solved.

> [Lack of information and accounting] would plunge most organizations in the private sector into a quick and merciful liquidation.

Groups . . . at the local level certainly felt that the Israelites faced with the requirement to make bricks without straw had a comparatively routine and possible task.

If Florence Nightingale were carrying her lamp through the corridors of the NHS today she would almost certainly be searching for the people in charge.

Or consider the Vice President and Chairman of the Board at Philips talking in 1987 about how the company was altering to compete in world markets:

If a boat is competing in a race, both weather change and the tactics of opponents require strategic actions. Co-ordinating these factors into a winning strategy is a challenge that tests the sailor's skills. Those of us involved in international business activity have been experiencing heavy weather change . . .

(See also Chapter 20 on Verbal Skills.)

Finally be specific about your vision. Say what it would be like to visit your organization in a few months' or years' time, once your particular vision has been realized. Describe and explain, for example, how you would be serving your customers, what kind of meetings you would be holding, what the budget would look like, how people would be spending their time and so on.

GUIDELINES

- BUILD a word picture of the preferred future

- DEFINE core values and you will be close to expressing a vision of the future

- SEEK a vision which states deeply held beliefs in the preferred future and captures people's imagination

- JUDGE vision statements by whether they excite people, not whether they are practical

- AVOID numbers, long words and complicated sentences in vision statements

- USE words which bring colour and excitement to the language when describing the vision

- TALK about the vision using metaphors, word pictures, imagery, parables, analogies etc

- BE specific about your vision

- CONVERT vision to an action programme through communication, persistence, use of power, monitoring progress and rearranging how resources and people are used.

Strategies
4. Commitment

Sean Taylor came from Lancashire to lead a sales team that had already seen three other managers leave. When he talked about wanting to improve the team's performance he noticed how people glanced at each other. The body language said 'What's new? We've heard all this before'.

Unlike his predecessors, Sean's move to London was a major turning point in his career. He was utterly determined to get results and worked hard to communicate this to the team by the changes he tried.

The previous managers had treated the team as separate individuals who had to reach personal sales targets. Sean intended to scrap this divisive approach. Instead he wanted a single monthly sales target for the whole team with only an average figure available for each person as a guide to what needed to be achieved.

The early reaction to his proposal was opposition. Bonuses were geared to individual sales success and the best performers were reluctant to risk financial loss. Sean adjusted his proposals while sticking to his position of wanting the change. His transparently honest belief that the change made good sense eventually convinced the team. This and other actions which he took transformed the sales figures from pedestrian to outstanding. Sean demonstrated that to make things happen you need to be concerned about:

- Your personal commitment to chosen change actions, and

- The commitment of others in your organization.

Commitment to what?

Commitment means giving all of yourself while at work. When people are committed they:

- Make suggestions

- Attend to detail

43

- Welcome change

- Enjoy their job

- Are willing to try something new

- Have pride in their work and abilities

- Develop their talents and abilities

- Make every minute at work useful

- Get it right first time

- Co-operate with others

- Are trustworthy

- Constantly seek improvement

- Show loyalty

- Make that extra effort

- Acknowledge others' contributions.

Concern with building personal and workforce commitment has been growing ever since the Japanese began creating committed workforces everywhere they went.

Consultants Peter Martin and John Nicholls, who have made a special study of workforce involvement, suggest that there are three major pillars of commitment: a sense of belonging to the organization; a sense of excitement; and confidence in management (see Chart 10).

Belonging builds the essential loyalty necessary to overcome barriers of 'them and us'. Creating a sense of excitement motivates people to perform; and confidence in management provides the right climate for commitment to flourish.

Your commitment

It is not always easy to become committed to work goals, especially if they are not entirely your own. How do you switch on the inner fire, that sense of determination that tears you from your desk,

Chart 10

Creating commitment

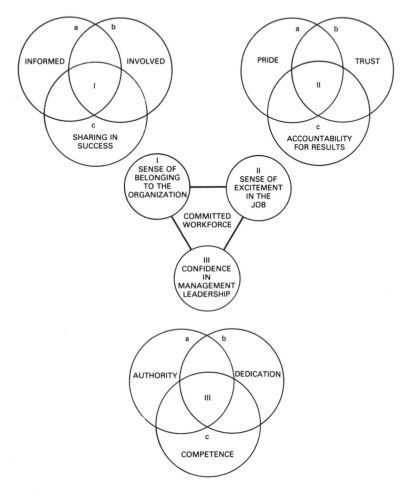

Source: Creating a Committed Work Force, Martin P, Nicholls J, IPM, 1987

making you hungry to lead change? If you already possess that burning inner drive this section of *Effective Change* will not tell you much you do not already know.

To create a commitment in others you must show that you have it yourself. Few people are convincing when riddled with doubts.

A commitment to change is not merely saying you are in favour of altering the *status quo*, it is being willing to put yourself out to achieve it.

The extent of your personal commitment to a particular change effort will often be decisive. People can tell when managers express commitment verbally without demonstrating it by their actions. For instance, managers who talk glibly of being committed to 'quality' must do more than create quality circles and hope that this will work. They have to be thoroughly immersed in all aspects of the issue, their personal commitment must permeate everything they touch. Similarly, technical innovation often fails because managers do not have sufficient long term commitment, the amount required being considerable.

When you are genuinely committed to a particular course of action and openly express the strength of your feelings, without undue aggression, this can be an extremely powerful force for change. Not only do people become infected with your confidence, they will often be swayed by your sheer persistence:

**A committed manager, armed with clear arguments
and mobilized support, can be unstoppable.**

If you find it difficult to feel the kind of commitment being described here try a version of the Chinese proverb that says you can eat anything if sliced up small enough. Find some aspect of your work or current goals, no matter how small, with which you can genuinely identify and which seems worth striving for. Keep breaking down the job or goal until you uncover some aspect relating to change that makes you feel excited, proud, interested, accountable – wanting results.

Committed managers have a thorough understanding of the final goal, they are crystal clear about what they want to achieve and can express it in simple everyday language. They can readily communicate what success (or failure) would look like; what benefits will flow from the change; what is needed to make it happen; and they are willing to fight hard for the necessary resources. They are often stubbornly unrealistic about likely obstacles, which they overcome despite the scepticism of less committed colleagues.

Persistence underpins commitment

Have you ever prized up a reluctant floor board, or experienced the frustration of attempting to open a large packing case and finding that nothing seemed to work? Tried turning a rusty screw and wondered whether it would ever come out? Anyone with these experiences knows that not all tools work immediately. It may take persistence before what you want to achieve finally yields to your efforts. Levers of change in organizations are much the same. You cannot be sure that the particular change action you use will work instantly:

**Commitment to change is a lever
which turns on the fulcrum of persistence.**

Malcolm Bryant, for example, was a director of a small advertising agency which handled the recruitment advertising for a large local authority. The account was worth several hundred thousand pounds. Everything Malcolm's agency placed in the media passed through the council's central personnel department. The latter allowed Malcolm little opportunity to produce visually attractive and more effective job advertisements.

Committed to producing high quality advertisements, Malcolm regularly suggested new ways of approaching the recruitment job but the central personnel people rejected the ideas. They were happy with mere lineage, arguing that it was cheap. One day Malcolm sent a copy of his latest proposals straight to a director of one of the council's main service departments, his real customer, though strictly he should not have done so. A series of meetings followed with this particular director who insisted on running the new and more effective approach. From then on the stifling effects of the central personnel department declined, and later one of the advertisements collected an industry award for effectiveness.

The experience of successful leaders of change results are produced by underpinning commitment with dogged persistence. Refusing to retreat in the face of organizational inertia or opposition, or going for the quick fix, is crucial to leading change.

Peter Blundel, for instance, a newly appointed chief executive in a large service organization, believed strongly that many employees possessed valuable ideas and ways of contributing to success. They were, however, often prevented from realizing their potential. Promoting equal opportunities was high on his personal agenda. Shortly after his arrival a group of women employees complained to him about the behaviour of a particular senior manager. This man treated women employees in ways that Peter was determined to eradicate. 'You'll never make things different around here unless you get rid of him,' they told him.

Other staff confirmed these opinions and Peter faced pressure to sack the manager in question. He refused. Summoning the manager he asked whether he was aware of how people felt about his behaviour. The man expressed surprise, promising to reform. Six months later Peter Blundel learned that matters had not improved and he forced the man's resignation. Despite the delay Blundel's actions had considerable effect. His commitment to equal opportunities was recognized and knowledge of his persistence in acting fairly, even to those under a cloud, quickly circulated throughout the entire organization. He had also demonstrated a consistency of focus, an ability to maintain the organization's direction, despite pressure to act in ways which would have undermined his change effort.

Persistence also underpinned Jason Bentley's commitment as the manager of a small section in a large, decentralized organization. His section supplied technical information. Being committed to providing an excellent service he decided that his section needed a microcomputer to develop advanced ways of handling information. Despite the need, his requests for resources received no priority.

Jason's reaction was to borrow a micro regularly from a work colleague using it to circulate new types of information. On the written material he conspicuously acknowledged the use of the loaned machine. Gradually, he was asked to produce more of the information for different people, and each time he made the point that it was being produced 'on a borrowed machine'. Finally at one meeting a senior manager asked for some data in a hurry and Jason replied cautiously that it all depended on whether he could get access to the computer. His persistence worked – he obtained his micro.

Others' commitment

'Truly involved people can do anything!' argues international management consultant Tom Peters who confesses to being 'frustrated to the point of rage' about the failure of managers to understand the need to obtain employee commitment through involvement.

Creating a commitment to change in others does not rely only on inner strength or personal powers of persuasion. There are other important ways of generating commitment and people's support for change. Involvement is merely one of the key elements in the three Pillars of Commitment described by Martin and Nicholls:

- A sense of belonging occurs when managers INFORM; INVOLVE; SHARE SUCCESS

- A sense of excitement depends on PRIDE; TRUST; ACCOUNT-ABILITY FOR RESULTS

- Confidence in leadership occurs when managers EXERT AUTHORITY; SHOW DEDICATION; DISPLAY CONFIDENCE.

There are numerous ways to follow through on the above, which is really a route map for gaining commitment (see Chart 10).

Commitment plans

To obtain other people's commitment to a specific change it is sometimes worth devising a commitment plan by completing the answers to these sentences:

- The situation I specifically want to change is ....

- The people to convince whose support (or lack of opposition) is needed are ....

- To gain their commitment the detailed steps I will take are ....

- To monitor that the situation keeps moving towards the desired end state I will ....

The first of these statements encourages you to express clearly the change objectives. The second identifies people who can help and those who can throw rocks in the way. They can seldom be answered quickly. You may have to work hard to understand the feelings and motivations of other people, to gauge the best way of gaining their commitment. Sometimes you may have to compromise, accepting that the most you can achieve is that they will not block your proposals.

Agreement is not commitment. Even when people agree to changes you cannot expect everyone to be committed to them; there is a spectrum of support for change:

COMMITMENT

TOTAL .... HIGH .... MEDIUM .... LOW .... NONE

On the left of the spectrum there is you, the leader of change, who is totally or at least highly committed to a particular change effort. Other people may be anywhere to the right of you along this spectrum. The commitment plan requires that you discover where they are on this spectrum and then find ways to:

- Minimize or eliminate their opposition

- Move them towards your position.

Inexperienced managers who want to make things happen often mistakenly expect other people to be closer to their position than they actually are, or to be willing to move when they are not. Because some people are not close to your position or are unwilling to move does not mean that the change effort is doomed. There is always a Critical Mass of people whose commitment will provide the leverage for action. The number of such people who constitute a Critical Mass will be relatively small yet crucial to success. The exact number may be unclear since it is made up of opinion moulders. The latter are not always obvious. Decide who is needed for a Critical Mass of commitment and direct your plans initially at them.

Incrementalism

Incrementalism is how many successful organizations gain commitment to large shifts; it is step-by-step change which will:

- DISGUISE intentions

- CREATE awareness

- DEVELOP value changes

- PRODUCE facts to help convince people

- BUILD consensus

- MAKE dealing with complexity manageable.

Many managers like incrementalism because they realize that early decisions made before commitment and information are available can be damaging, particularly if made under stress conditions. Those with a good record of leading change do not seek major agreements in the broad, formative stage of the change process. Instead the situation is acknowledged as tentative and subject to later review.

Incrementalism is not just muddling through. The elements of the process may be highly logical with concrete decisions being made on individual stages to gain commitment while leaving the final picture to the last possible minute.

With incrementalism managers can create pockets of commitment to their ideas. Projects are explored, options remain open and managers are opportunistic about building small, isolated commitments into a more powerful force.

This step-by-step approach may sometimes be concentrated in a very short period so that proposals are rapidly agreed and commitment fuelled by a sense of urgency and excitement.

Team building

Team building also generates organization-wide commitment to a change. It focusses on goals and;

- CREATES a climate of social support for change

- OPENS up the communication process

- GAINS commitment to decisions

- HELPS achieve individual as well as organizational goals

- BUILDS interdependence and team effort.

Leading change by team building is a slow process, sometimes taking years before the full benefits are realized. It is seldom relied upon as the sole change mechanism (see also Chapter 19 on Team Building).

GUIDELINES

- CREATE a specific commitment plan to show how you will build support for your ideas

- IDENTIFY groups or individuals whose support is needed

- DEVELOP a strategy for gaining other people's commitment to change

- DECIDE on the Critical Mass of support

- BECOME unstoppable by being committed, armed with clear arguments and mobilized support

- SHOW a thorough understanding of what the final goal is all about

- UNDERPIN commitment with persistence

- CREATE a sense of belonging by informing, involving and sharing success

- GENERATE excitement by developing trust, pride in and accountability for results

- OBTAIN confidence in your leadership by exerting your authority, showing dedication and displaying confidence

- USE incrementalism to gain support

- TEAM BUILD to create long term support for change.

Strategies
5. Simplify

Sherlock Holmes always looked 'for the simplest solution' to a crime. The approach is equally relevant to the management of change. Highly successful change makers have learned how to simplify complex issues, reducing them to do-able tasks. KISS, or 'KEEP IT SIMPLE – STUPID!' remains a useful criterion by which to judge change actions.

Complexity is loved by some organizations and is often presented as a sign of sophisticated thinking. In fact complexity, particularly of reports, systems, procedures and structures, is more usually a sign of confusion and woolly thinking. The drive to simplify is a search for clarity. Only by simplifying can the average manager make sense of what needs to be done and how to do it.

In successful organizations this drive to simplify surfaces in numerous ways. For example there is the proverbial insistence of Proctor and Gamble and other large organizations that no memo should be more than one page in length, no report more than four or five pages. Word processors stimulate the production of long communications and reports. Because all his staff had their own desk top computers, for instance, President of Apple Computer John Sculley received what amounted to a stream of consciousness in correspondence. He too insisted that ideas, proposals and reports be reduced to one page only. This may appear to be nit-picking, but in practice it promotes clarity and precision.

Simplifying makes the unmanageable manageable, reducing things to understandable chunks. When people grasp what you are trying to achieve there is a better chance that your ideas will be accepted, with less resistance and more tolerance of the consequences. Angela Miller, for instance, was a senior manager in charge of local services for physically disabled people. She was concerned at how a large day centre for disabled people operated. It had a troubled history, the previous manager having been retired early. The past dominated the thinking of the centre's employees. Little new appeared to be happening. The acting manager complained about lack of support for change and was unhappy about his temporary role.

Angela tackled the complex task of turning the centre around by simplifying what needed to be done. Calling the staff team together she asked each person to write down a personal balance sheet of positive and negative points about the centre. Their lists were lengthy, revealing just how much needed to be done. Angela added her own list and then worked with the team to turn the material into what they called The Ten Point Challenge.

The ten point plan was converted into simple tasks spread over two years which would guide the Centre's development. These simple ideas fired everyone's imagination and enthusiasm. For the first time there was a clear focus for action. The Ten Points were posted on a wall and were referred to regularly. Everybody knew and understood what was being attempted and what each person had to do. When doubts arose or confidence slipped the 'ten commandments', as they soon came to be called, were used and this encouraged acceptance of some of the inevitable strains that the changes caused.

By keeping change actions simple you limit complexity and confusion. Simplifying improves the chances that what you want to happen actually does. Napoleon reduced his complex battle plans to instructions that his generals could all understand. On his staff he retained a man known as 'Napoleon's idiot' who read the plans and explained them back to the emperor. Napoleon reasoned that if this none too bright soldier understood them so would his generals!

Simplification does not mean ignoring complexity. For instance, when the AIDS virus began causing concern policy makers, health and social services managers and others over-simplified the situation, and underestimated the scale of resources needed. Henry Ford did the same when he offered his customers any colour 'as long as it's black'.

Choices

When proposals are being discussed a series of options are often presented. Although this is widely regarded as good practice:

Simplify the choices.

Limit options to the most important ones. In a report or presentation it is unhelpful to be offered a dozen different ways of achieving some aim. Even if each has been carefully evaluated few people have the inclination to review all the arguments. What matters is reducing the choices to two or three well argued ones. Relegate the rest to an appendix or a verbal aside in your presentation.

Presenting people with more than a few options makes them feel powerless, unable to understand or control events:

People are de-powered by too many choices.

Simplification runs deep in many of the world's most successful enterprises. Almost all quality improvements, for example, stem from simplification of design, manufacturing, layout, procedures and so on. The Japanese genius for miniaturization and building in quality is based on a passion for simplification and the elimination of wasteful expenditure.

Management information systems, particularly financial ones, are common purveyors of complexity and frequently obstruct change because the very fact that there is a system gives managers the illusion that they understand what is happening. While the notion that you can run a global corporation on half a dozen key indicators is perhaps an exaggeration, few organizations can justify the mountain of material that is produced in the name of control. When you cannot predict what you are going to sell next month, or know where the resources went last month, then it's time to wield a knife on the monitoring output and get back to basics.

Simplifying objectives is another important area of change management. Objectives need to be expressed in simple terms, and kept down to perhaps one or two in number. Some organizations expect each manager to have a dozen or so objectives and end up with hundreds which cannot be properly monitored nor related back to a strategic aim. More important than a dozen objectives is a simple, intelligible sense of direction.

One area increasingly subject to simplification is organizational structure. Instead of an enterprise becoming ever larger and more complex there is a conscious decision to keep it simple by networking, or what has also been called spin offs. As parts of the organization grow and develop, individual employees are encouraged to break away and start their own enterprise. The 'mother firm' may even finance the development. A network of interdependencies is created in which those with the necessary drive and creativity are given their head to develop businesses of their own.

The original concept of networking began in the Xerox Corporation and has spread particularly in the high technology industries such as computers. The spin offs allow the main organization to keep its own structure simple while spawning an ever more complex range of linkages which are mutually profitable.

Small steps

The more complex a change situation the more it will gain from simplification and:

Division into small, manageable steps.

The average car weighs half a ton. Insert a jack underneath and even a weakling can soon have the front wheels off the ground. The jack reduces the lifting job to a series of small steps, like a steady ratchet movement of a handle back and forth. These small movements ultimately produce a large effect. Many organizational change actions work the same way. They too are based on simplifying the task into a series of small steps which cumulate in a large impact.

Dividing the change effort into a series of small actions can get your foot in the door. You persuade people to agree a tiny step in the direction you want to go; eventually, based on the success of the previous steps, they may be willing to take more or bigger ones.

The popularity of the small step approach is sometimes used wrongly to justify maintaining the *status quo* and block urgently needed change. For example, some years ago the American Ford Motor Company invented a vastly improved method of rust proofing car bodies. The steel was given a positive electrical charge and the paint a negative one. When the body was dipped in paint every centimetre of metal work was successfully coated. The invention was too revolutionary for many Ford managers to accept and the cost of converting dozens of factories to the new system overwhelmed them. Despite the advancing Japanese competition the board of Directors were only persuaded to introduce the new system in a step-by-step approach, one factory at a time. Half way through the programme the company lost its technological lead and was forced to convert the remainder hurriedly just to stay competitive.

If used to block change the small step approach can demotivate the very people who early on pushed for the change as they see their proposals being given ritual support with little impetus for implementation.

The general approach of using small steps is the way many organizations initiate and control major change. Ultimately all radical change reduces to a series of small, manageable steps.

There is no universal agreement on how to simplify or break down the change sequence process itself into manageable stages. The sequence shown in Chapter 9 on Action Sequence suggests the stages that are most commonly used.

The search for simplification is endless, whether in cutting the layers of management to four or five, reducing head office staff to no more than a dozen people, creating manageable marketing plans that people understand, keeping reports to a maximum of five pages, eliminating components in a product or issuing instructions to an employee. Like motherhood few people would oppose the idea of simplifying things. The fact that it does not happen in so many places is due to lack of persistence and clarity of thought. It takes a determined, sustained effort before an organization builds simplification into its corporate thinking as a route to effective change.

GUIDELINES

- JUDGE change actions by whether they are simple to understand and do

- SIMPLIFY choices by limiting options

- DIVIDE change programmes into small, manageable steps

- SEARCH continuously for ways to simplify

- LIMIT objectives to just one or two, focus more on direction.

Strategies
6. Power and influence

Long before Machiavelli started his management consultancy to princes in distress, power was a dirty word. Managers seldom discuss it openly. Those who do are usually people who feel powerless, rather than those who already have it.

Politics and power are loaded words: those who understand the former and possess the latter seldom use the terms. We have become expert instead at avoiding the words 'managerial power' by using another language:

- Let managers manage

- He's very influential

- He's got real clout

- Carries weight with the chairman

- She's tough minded

- She's obstructive

- He can be difficult

- Has the Director's ear

- You'll need to persuade . . .

- You keep hearing her name mentioned

- She is very persuasive

- There's a lot of politics here

- She is very controlling

- He has access to a lot of resources

- Everybody goes to her for advice.

In fact talking about your management power may well produce embarrassment or a response as if you are revealing your sex life. What then is power? At its simplest it is the ability to induce or influence behaviour. As no single explanation seems to satisfy everyone, the following meaning is used here:

Power is a measure of your potential to:

Get others to do what you want them to do or

Avoid being forced by others to do what you don't want to do.

Power is what you give other people. That is to say, people acquire authority to get others to do what they want them to do mainly because those people are *willing* to let them exercise power. An example of this is when a new manager joins an organization; in the early days people may be unwilling to argue with or oppose this new person whose power to make things happen is not yet known. Thus in the first six months the new manager may be able to exercise more influence in making significant changes than at a later stage when he is well established.

The most effective managers are not always those who are the most pleasant or have the strongest need to achieve change. Research shows that the most effective managers are the ones who have a high need for power, are highly self controlled and who channel their power into socially desirable directions. This means involving subordinates in shared or collaborative approaches rather than appearing to dominate and control everything.

Nor is power a fixed quantity, although there may be a limit to how much one person can acquire. Managerial power can be likened to a plant that needs cultivating – depending on what fertilizer you use and how it is applied the faster the growth can be.

Major organizational change is in one sense revolutionary. It is overturning the *status quo*, creating a new reality with new relationships, roles and objectives. Power is certainly a crucial component, as some major changes can only be achieved through using power and authority to compel compliance. Neither power nor formal planning systems, however, fully explain how strategic change occurs.

Since power is certainly essential for achieving major change most managers want it, even if they seldom admit to the fact. As a first step in trying to expand your power you need to ask 'How much power do I have at present?'

Checking out your power

To check out your power consider your present situation. For instance, how sensitive are you to where power exists in your organization? It is easy to point to a senior manager and say that he or she has a lot of power. The reality is that less senior people can also acquire considerable power without being in a high status role.

Margaret Allen was a personnel officer in a local government department, seconded there from the central personnel service. Officially she reported to the head of the personnel service, but in practice she was so embedded in the department to which she had been seconded that she had almost a free hand. She gained the trust of the department and gradually managers at all levels came to ask for her advice. They even joked about going to see 'Aunty Marge'. By the time she retired Margaret had acquired power in the department far beyond her formal job description.

Thus, in reviewing your own power position, do not assume that being in a junior position is necessarily a reason for preventing you from gaining power and influence.

Managers who do succeed at gaining power are usually extremely sensitive to where power exists in their organization. They are alert to who has influence on whom and how. In considering your own power position, review who, in your organization, seems to make things happen, regardless of their position in the formal structure. Identifying who has the power takes you half way to discovering how to turn it to your own account.

Increasing your own power is like any other kind of investment. You may have to take calculated risks with your initial supply, investing it in activities and decisions which will produce a return in terms of added power. For example, Maurice Jones was a middle manager in a company that needed to improve its record on equal opportunities. Top management created a committee to make proposals and to see through the necessary changes.

Other managers saw the subject as uncongenial because no one really knew how much commitment to improving equal opportunities was really being made by the top management. Despite these risks, Maurice Jones offered to chair the new committee and once appointed set about organizing an in-house survey. On behalf of the committee he presented the results to top management. Though the survey findings were not particularly congenial, the presentation raised Maurice's personal profile in the organization and whenever issues to do with equal opportunity were being discussed he tended to be invited to attend.

When the committee reported its proposals for change Maurice again played a prominent role and was asked to lead the next phase of implementation. This covered a wide variety of the company's areas of operation; there were soon several project groups created and Maurice was asked to help steer their activities. Within a year Maurice had acquired considerable power and influence, gaining the ear of several top managers and improving his own personal chances of promotion.

Has your career path moved you towards key sources of power in the organization? When thinking about your next career move give some thought to whether it takes you closer to where the power lies, as well as whether it is better paid or more interesting. Anyone posted abroad from a large company soon comes to realize their increased isolation and vulnerability. The lines of communication with those in power are extended and perhaps weakened. More than one manager has done extremely well in a foreign posting only to return home to find that they have been away too long from those in real power and that their future prospects are now worse, not better.

Do you use your power to influence and manage people upon whom you are dependent? There is little point in gaining power if you do not exercise it to get things done. People need to see your power in action to help them do their jobs better. Successfully using your power and influence to achieve an objective has a multiplier effect. Power used well leads to gaining more power.

Do people see you as powerful and influential? One way of gaining increased power and influence is to convince others that you already have a considerable amount. Putting this across is what leadership is about and why personality is so crucial.

Finally, do you really recognize that all your actions can affect your power? Like Maurice Jones, mentioned above, managers with power tend to have a high visibility in the organization. The greater your visibility the more likely that anything you do will directly or indirectly affect your power. What meetings you attend, who you have lunch with, who you ask for help can all have an impact.

By the same token, it is important to avoid any actions which could accidentally decrease your power and influence. Powerful managers tend to pick objectives carefully and make sure they are both desirable and attainable. They avoid fighting battles they cannot win.

Suppose, for example, that you are a manager charged with introducing a computerized personnel information system. You will quickly discover that one option for creating the new system is linking with the organization's payroll package. Such a move, though, may meet stiff resistance from the financial experts, concerned to protect their system from contamination. In this situation, a predictable way to lose power is to insist that the new personnel system cannot happen without being linked with the payroll. Such an insistence may eventually kill the project which will also affect your power and influence. Even if you win the argument it may permanently damage your relationships with powerful connections elsewhere in the organization.

Types of power

Managers possess several kinds of power, using them at different times in varying quantities. You can get things done and achieve change through:

- COERCIVE POWER – making things happen by fear, threats or punishment

- EXPERTISE – others comply because of your knowledge or skills

- ROLE POSITION – use of authority from your job or location in the organization; includes control of important resources

- REWARDS – ability to reward emotionally and financially; includes the persuasive skills associated with leadership and personality

- CONNECTIONS – access to networks, membership of groups in and out of the organization and hence social power. Establishing favourable relationships is based on:

    Creating a sense of obligation
    Developing a strong professional reputation
    Identification of others with the manager
    Perceived dependence.

In thinking about your own power it is thus worth reviewing:

On what is my present power based?

Dependency

In understanding power and then using it for achieving change, every manager should be aware of dependency.

The more power you acquire the more likely you will become dependent on other people. As the above definition of power suggests, an ability to get others to do things also means being dependent on their efforts. This experience of increasing dependency on others can be puzzling and indeed frustrating, particularly for newer managers who have perhaps trained in a narrow professional area and are now gaining wider responsibilities.

Instead of promotion ensuring that you can get more things done and quicker, you may find that the reverse is true. Because you no longer do everything yourself, changes take even longer to produce than before. The extent of management dependency is often not recognized. You may, for example, be dependent on:

- Your boss

- Your boss's boss

- Your peer group

- Unions

- Subordinates

- Subordinates of subordinates

- Customers

- Suppliers

- Competitors

- Statutory bodies

- Community organizations.

The need for power is thus more to do with handling dependency than being power hungry or the urge to get ahead. Your job demands that you plan, organize, budget and control, yet it does not automatically supply the right amount of authority to achieve these ends. Your dependency on other people is always greater than the power and control inherent in your job or position.

The number of people on whom a manager is dependent and over whom no direct authority is exercised, has steadily risen. In one Japanese bank, for example, in defiance of neat theories about span of control, one manager has several hundred branch managers reporting directly to him. Similarly, the number of people who can affect a manager's performance has tended to increase. The first basic lesson emerging from the reality of dependency is:

Identify those on whom you are most dependent.

This means being willing to acknowledge your dependency, not acting as if you are the only source of authority to get things done. Indeed one of the quickest ways to lose power and influence is to act as if you are always the prime mover, the principal source of ideas, or the only person who really gets results. The second lesson from the reality of dependency is:

**Broaden your support so that when you need help
it can be obtained from multiple sources.**

Networking is the ability to create an interlinked group of people who have things in common and who assist one another in getting things done. These may be contacts, personal connections and other linkages on which you can call. You can widen your support in various other ways, including creating obligations. This may involve looking for opportunities to do favours for certain people, helping them when they have a problem, being willing to share knowledge and information and so on.

Research into how power is actually used by successful managers also provides some practical suggestions for action.

First, managers controlling resources valued by others or seen as being important tend to use a greater variety of influence strategies than those with less power. The practical lessons from this are:

**Examine closely whether you are relying too much on
one strategy for achieving change.**

**Explore ways to widen the variety of influence strategies
and tactics used in exercising power.**

How could you go about developing a more varied approach to using influence? You will tend to use one of the following tactics to make things happen:

- Reason

- Friendliness

- Creating coalitions

- Bargaining

- Assertiveness

- Relying on higher authority

- Sanctions.

While using a mixture of tactics, successful change makers do not attempt to use them all. They tend to rely heavily on skills and knowledge combined with reason to make things happen. Less experienced managers try using all seven approaches to gain influence, but as a result they usually complete fewer objectives and are probably using these tactics indiscriminately.

Secondly, managers with power use assertiveness more frequently than those with less power. Assertiveness is based more on personality and leadership skills than possession of organizational power. The lessons for practical action are:

Gaining power means being willing to be assertive, and

Being assertive will often attract power.

See also Assertiveness in Chapter 20 on Verbal Skills.

Widening your influence

Since power and influence are hard to measure, increasing them may seem purely a matter of management flair and leadership skills. But it is possible to be rather more systematic in analysing the factors that lead to increased influence.

You can conduct a Circles of Influence exercise either on your own or with your management team. When done properly it takes about an hour and teases out new ways of tackling what sometimes are apparently insoluble problems.

On a large sheet of paper or a flip chart draw three circles as shown in Chart 11. Circle A contains problems that either you or your team can solve completely with no outside assistance. Circle B contains problems over which either you or your team have influence without complete control. Finally, Circle C contains problems or forces affecting you or the team that are completely outside your influence.

Chart 11

Circles of influence diagram

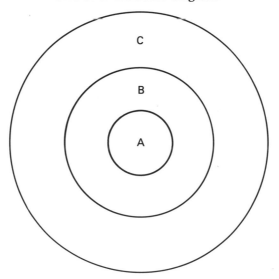

A Circles of Influence analysis can be carried out by following the steps shown in Box 10. The final step can produce surprising revelations, challenging the negative idea that you or the team are powerless over a particular situation. Instead, you begin inventing ways of taking back power and acquiring influence where before you felt that you had little or none.

Box 10

> ### *Circles of influence exercise*
>
> *Step 1*   Spend ten minutes listing the problems currently causing concern. If you do this with your team, each member writes down their own particular list.
>
> *Step 2*   Once the problem list is completed it is written on a flip chart. If there are several lists these are combined to eliminate duplications. Each problem is clarified to avoid vagueness.
>
> *Step 3*   Review each problem to decide in which circle of influence it falls. If a team does the exercise there has to be consensus on each problem as to where it falls in the circles. The problem is recorded on the diagram by a brief title or code letter.
>
> *Step 4*   The final stage is the creative one. You, or the team, try to think of ways of extending the boundaries of circles A and B to increase your influence over the forces that are affecting the situation. You ask: 'How could we move an item from further out to further in?'

GUIDELINES

- IDENTIFY your own power skills

- ANALYSE whether your career path is moving you towards key sources of power in the organization

- USE your power to influence and manage those on whom you are dependent

- ASSESS whether others see you as powerful and influential and if not why not

- ASSUME that all your actions can affect your power; avoid actions which can accidentally decrease it

- RECOGNIZE that the greater your power the more you will be dependent on others

- SEEK power to handle dependency

- IDENTIFY those on whom you are most dependent

- BROADEN your support so that when you need help it can be obtained from multiple sources

- EXAMINE whether you are over-reliant on one strategy of influence for achieving change

- USE assertiveness to gain power

- CONDUCT a Circles of Influence exercise to analyse how to extend influence

- CHECK who has the power and is dependent on whom

- SEEK ways to gain control over tangible resources, such as budgets, people, buildings and equipment

- FIND ways to control useful information and information channels

- SPEND time developing relationships and gathering information; take low cost, high pay-off actions first.

Strategies
7. Resistance to change

In 1981 Rupert Murdoch acquired *The Times* and *The Sunday Times* from the Thomson Organization. On meeting Harold Evans, *The Sunday Times'* Editor, he told him: 'I'm going to make a clean sweep of management. I'm fixing the redundancies tomorrow'.

Murdoch used a blunt instrument because he had no faith in the existing management team and wanted anyone who could resist the changes out of the way. Some years later when introducing major technological change into his newspapers he sacked the entire printing staff which led to the famous Wapping siege. Once again he was ruthless in dealing with resistance.

Being ruthless, or even merely determined, is still no guarantee of overcoming resistance. For instance, British Leyland, British Steel and British Airways all acquired strong managers bent on change. Each had great difficulties in radically affecting their organization's strongly held values. There was enormous resistance against altering BL's centralized, production orientated approach; British Steel's narrow non-market approach; and BA's low commitment to customer service.

In the case of British Airways, for instance, the scale of investment needed to tackle the problem has run into millions of pounds, involving countless hours of retraining, new reward systems and a realization that it requires years not months to overcome the inertia and resistance uncovered. As Machiavelli long ago observed 'there is nothing more difficult to carry out nor doubtful of success nor more dangerous to handle than to initiate a new order of things'.

Resistance is so common that it is a part of the change process which all managers need to know about and have ideas on how to deal with.

Resistance is:

> **Any conduct that tries to maintain the *status quo***
> **in the face of pressure to change it.**

The *status quo* is thus the pivot on which resistance revolves. When trade unions, for example, are mistrustful of proposals their concern is usually with the extent to which the *status quo* will alter, who will be affected and how.

When one thinks of trade unions, one usually thinks of resistance as a form of active opposition, perhaps involving go slows, walk outs and strikes. The word sabotage in fact comes from the word sabot or shoe. At the start of the industrial revolution French workers were known to throw their sabots – shoes – into the machine to destroy the mechanization of their work places. Yet, equally, resistance can be passive, showing itself when employees are demoralized, demotivated and unwilling to co-operate in a constructive way to support change.

When managers seek change they are seldom merely tinkering with tangibles like machinery. They are also directly or indirectly affecting the ongoing processes within the organization. These processes may well involve relationships such as who reports to whom, who has contact with whom and so on. Interfering with such relationships may generate conflict and hence resistance.

Types

When trying to make things happen you are likely to meet various kinds of resistance such as:

- Cultural

- Social

- Organizational

- Psychological.

Cultural resistance occurs when the values which are built into the organization are affected. People live by these values, and in some organizations it may be important to preserve face. Changes which do not allow this may generate both conflict and resistance. The organization may have certain traditions which for years people have accepted and in some cases planned their life around. An example of this is where it has become custom and practice for someone to be sent on specialized training after being in a particular job for several years. On their return the expectation may be that they will then gain further promotion. If management decides .hat this tradition is no longer efficient or justified there may be considerable repercussions in trying to alter it.

Social resistance happens when changes threaten to affect relationships. For instance, the changes may appear to damage group solidarity or teamwork which people want to protect. Or perhaps the changes challenge conformity to existing norms. It may, for example, be accepted tradition that the organization does not impinge on people's holidays and weekends. A manager who decides to hold training sessions at the weekend may meet considerable opposition.

Organizational resistance takes place when the changes seem likely to interfere with formal arrangements which people have come to accept as the *status quo*; for example, when the changes seem to affect status differentials, or impact on who is where in the hierarchy. It may also arise when the changes seem likely to alter or threaten certain people's power and influence.

Psychological resistance involves selective perception. Change is seen as detrimental, not beneficial, which leads to conservatism and conformity.

While you may not always know which type of resistance you are meeting, and the above classification does not really explain why it occurs, knowing about the different types of resistance can be a useful tool for starting to analyse the issues.

Another useful way of analysing resistance is to consider its:

- Intensity

- Source

- Focus.

Try and judge the intensity of resistance since this may offer a guide as to how you should respond, and indeed whether you may hope to overcome it and how long that might take.

The source of resistance is sometimes hard to judge. There are often many hidden agendas. People are influenced by values, facts and beliefs so that uncovering the source may be helpful in developing a strategy for suitable action.

The focus or location of the resistance could be within you, in other people or in the work environment.

There are as many reasons why resistance arises as there are managers. Broadly though the reasons can be reduced to:

Behavioural factors such as emotional reasons

Rational or system factors.

Each situation generates its own set of circumstance. Box 11 identifies some of the better known general causes. Resistance to technological innovation has also been the subject of considerable research in recent years and some of the causes are shown in Box 12. The commonest reason for resisting technological change is perhaps management's psychological and emotional mind set. This stems from a reluctance to make mistakes, a belief that a new idea or product must be as successful or profitable as the current winner on which the firm has grown.

Box 11

Why people resist change in organizations

- A desire not to lose something of value – insecurity; advancement

- Historical factors – how previous changes have been handled

- How the change is being handled

- Misunderstanding of the change and its implications – lack of information; no perceived benefits

- Beliefs that the change does not make sense for the organization

- Uncertainty about how much freedom there is to do things differently

- Lack of decision-making skills

- Inexperience of implementing change; reluctance to experiment

- Existing psychological and social commitments to current products, processes and organizations; strong peer group norms

- Complacency

- Powerful trade union attitudes to change methods

- Complexity – frustration caused by technical problems; fear of uncertainty

- Management wants change – therefore resist it!

Box 12

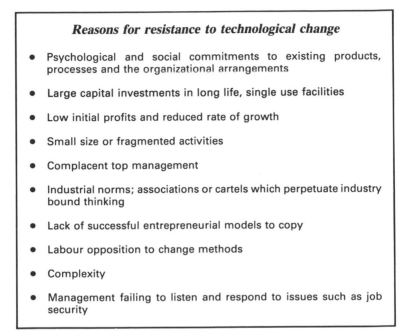

Reasons for resistance to technological change

- Psychological and social commitments to existing products, processes and the organizational arrangements

- Large capital investments in long life, single use facilities

- Low initial profits and reduced rate of growth

- Small size or fragmented activities

- Complacent top management

- Industrial norms; associations or cartels which perpetuate industry bound thinking

- Lack of successful entrepreneurial models to copy

- Labour opposition to change methods

- Complexity

- Management failing to listen and respond to issues such as job security

Coming to terms with resistance

Understandably many managers consider resistance to their proposals with distaste; opposition is seen as a negative force creating unwelcome obstacles. This interpretation of resistance is increasingly being questioned.

First, there are those who would advocate abandoning altogether the concept of resistance. Being such an all embracing term it hardly helps matters except to provide a rather fuzzy label for a set of complex behaviours. It fails to reveal, for instance, why on some days people may be enthusiastic for change yet resist it on other days; and it makes no allowance for the fact that today's resisters may be tomorrow's supporters.

Secondly, some people, particularly psychologists who have studied the problem of resistance in some depth, have argued that resistance to organizational change is perfectly rational rather than merely irrational. Why people resist change suggests that, from their standpoint, resistance may be exactly the right thing correctly based on self interest. It may even be in the interest of the organization itself.

So resistance can be seen as a positive asset. By challenging assumptions it helps stimulate the development of mutually acceptable goals. Instead of managers simply announcing the end result they intend to achieve, resistance may modify it and in the process make it more realistic and acceptable.

Resistance to change can also help to prevent stagnation. For instance, when a trade union challenges certain management changes it may throw light on far more fundamental issues that need addressing, such as the effects on the quality of the product or the service being provided by the organization. In opposing shipyard closures, for example, unions have often sought to draw management's attention to new or neglected market opportunities or new ways to reduce costs.

Resistance also stimulates curiosity, allowing problems to be aired and alternative solutions to be discussed. It can be a necessary cost of personal and social change. Thus a balanced view of resistance reveals that it is not always counter-productive nor to be opposed at all costs. It is part of the normal checks and balances within an organization, and in many cases can be considered a healthy element protecting the *status quo*.

A good example of this happening occurred when a manager in a local authority wanted to alter the arrangements in a number of buildings staffed by a mixture of manual and salaried staff. The new arrangements offered the opportunity for many of the manual workers to become salaried staff and from the management's viewpoint offered the chance to recruit higher calibre staff who would work more flexibly. There was considerable resistance from the trade unions to the proposals. Discussions revealed that the unions in fact liked the proposals. What they objected to was an arrangement in which certain long standing employees would have their existing jobs deleted and be asked to apply for the new jobs. Once the management agreed to allow people to choose for themselves, either to apply for the new jobs or to stay in their old ones, the resistance died.

Thus resistance may be thoroughly justified because the proposed changes are harmful in some way. It may force one to think more carefully about introducing change. It is easier to handle resistance if you see it as functional, not as a challenge to your authority and your ideas. It helps to ask:

What useful purpose is the resistance serving?

If you expect there to be resistance this can become a self-fulfilling prophecy. Act, instead, as if people will respond to change in a variety of ways, both positively and negatively.

Coping with resistance

Since resistance is so common how should managers go about coping with it? The first step is to:

Identify real or perceived negative consequences of the change.

Having analysed what factors are contributing to resistance:

**Weaken the apparent link between the change
and the negative consequences.**

People resist change because they see no personal pay-off and because they believe they, or something they value, will be adversely affected. Dealing with resistance means recognizing this and taking appropriate action.

Experienced managers often assume that they cannot eliminate resistance and that the main aim must be to reduce it to manageable proportions. Take for example Alfred Turner, the manager in charge of a large, privately run old people's home. He has three domestic cleaners on his staff and wants to alter the way that they organize their work so that one cleaner spends much of her time operating the laundry equipment. Two of the domestics will have to change the floor on which they work to make the plan succeed. He knows that they have become committed to working on their particular floor and take pride in the standard of cleanliness which they achieve. They will be reluctant to change to another floor.

Rather than simply instruct them and risk creating smouldering resentment he calls them together to discuss the problem. He shows them the total number of hours of cleaning available and the number of hours needed to run the laundry equipment and asks for their ideas. At first they sit back and look confused. With a bit more encouragement a lively discussion begins on ways of running the laundry equipment in a more sensible way than at present. Eventually one of the cleaners puts forward the plan Alfred already has in mind. There is no resistance.

Actions

You may often need to think in terms of actions to reduce rather than eliminate resistance. It may be avoided or at least reduced with these kinds of actions:

- Avoid surprises. People need time to come to terms with change. Let people think about proposals and they will be less inclined to automatically resist them

- Obtain top management support

- Provide information. Lack of information creates a vacuum which will be filled with conjectures, rumours and assumptions leading to increased resistance; replace with knowledge, particularly about personal payoffs from the change. Resisters may become allies

- Ensure participation. Make your changes their changes by enabling those affected to:

  have a stake in the change

  feel that some or all of the change is their own, not devised and operated by outsiders

  help diagnose the problem and feel its importance

  reach a group consensus in support

- Reduce, not increase burdens. People will support changes which help them rather than add to their problems

- Recognize feelings. It is essential to deal with the feelings aroused by a change which may threaten people in some way. Acknowledge valid objections and take steps to relieve unnecessary fears

- Incorporate values and ideals. If what you propose accords with the values and ideals of those affected they will be less likely to oppose what you want to do

- Offer new, worthwhile experiences

- Avoid threats to autonomy and security

- Be adaptable. Keep your project or plan open to revision or modification if experience suggests that alterations are desirable

- Neutral period. Offer a period during which employee work

performance cannot adversely affect personal income or other benefits

- New blood. New managers can often overcome resistance where older ones have failed. A new person has a good chance to sweep aside old ways of thinking and of doing things. The momentum may carry others along

- Convince opinion makers. Look for strategically placed people in pivotal positions and persuade them. They will carry others

- Pay the price of change. Be willing to bear the risks inherent in creative innovation. If managers are put on the defensive about their ideas, are penalized or are not rewarded for risk taking they will not commit themselves to change

- Set the stage for change. Managers should show a positive attitude to change and innovation, selling the idea of team effort; creating opportunities to learn and accept change

- Simplicity. Keep the change simple to understand

- Small steps. Introduce changes in small steps rather than one big one

- Compatibility. Try making the change fit the organizational environment as far as possible

- Timing. Avoid introducing change at an entirely inappropriate and inconvenient time such as Christmas or the New Year

- Informal leaders. Involve the informal leaders since this gives the programme credibility

- Avenues of appeal. Build into the change programme a formal route for appeal that eases upward communication from dissatisfied individuals.

This is not a comprehensive list of possible actions. As the Murdoch examples above showed it is also possible to adopt power strategies as a way of dealing with resistance. Coercion forces compliance and produces a low level of commitment to the change. However, in some cases managers may decide that compliance is all they require

A longer term strategy to deal with resistance to change is a re-education programme such as the one mentioned earlier in British Airways. This assumes that those on the receiving end are rational and will respond to facts and information, and is usually only feasible when change does not have to be immediate. Re-education can occur through extensive organizational development techniques, training and communication programmes and other information sharing methods. These usually start with establishing in everyone's mind a clear need for change. While re-education may prevent appeals to resist change from succeeding it is not a reliable way of achieving large scale change in the short run, particularly where motivation to change is low.

Another approach to minimizing resistance is through the technique of identification. You provide the people you want to influence with a living example of the behaviour which you want to promote. People learn by identifying with you and trying to be like you. For example, a manager who wants to encourage his subordinates to get closer to the customer has to be seen doing this too, spending time listening to what customers say and using the results to influence future actions.

By virtue of its existence, resistance brings people into conflict with managers wanting to make change. Handling conflict is therefore an important management skill. Managers deal with conflict in varying ways, the main ones being:

● AVOIDANCE – withdrawing from the conflict situation

● SMOOTHING – trying to cover up and pretend that everything is calm, co-operative and pleasant

● BARGAINING – compromising, inviting negotiation; each part gains and each part loses or gives up something

● FORCING – fighting a battle to see which party will be the winner; creates a win/lose situation

● PROBLEM SOLVING – confronting the issue; implies collaborative working not fighting amongst parties to solve the problem.

The last of these tends to be most productive although, depending on the power situation, both forcing and bargaining can also be effective. See also Chapter 20 on Verbal Skills and Chapter 6 on Power.

GUIDELINES

- IDENTIFY if possible the type of resistance you expect to meet: cultural; social; organizational; psychological

- ANALYSE resistance by: intensity; source; and focus

- LOOK for behavioural factors, such as emotional reasons for resistance, and rational or system factors

- VIEW resistance to organizational change as perfectly rational rather than irrational

- ASK what useful purpose the resistance is serving

- IDENTIFY real or perceived negative consequences of the change, then

- WEAKEN the apparent link between the change and the negative consequences

- REDUCE rather than eliminate resistance by measures such as avoiding surprises; obtaining top management support for the change; providing information; participation; and so on.

Procedures
8. Planning strategic change

John Sculley, one time president of Pepsi Cola, later president of Apple Computer, sees strategic planning in simple, easily understandable terms. 'We ask ourselves: what will the year 1992 be like? We create in our minds a visual portrait of what the economy, our industry and our company will look like. Then we move back into the present, envisioning what we have to do in small steps to get to the future. What do we have to do in 1989 for example to achieve our vision of 1992? We call this "back to the future planning".

Like many other managerial leaders, Sculley has little time for centralized formal planning systems. Everybody in Apple is expected to think about the future and the changes needed to make it real.

When, some years ago, John Welch became chairman of General Electric in the USA, the first thing he did was to dismantle most of the company's strategic planning department. A review of the last 20 years revealed that each of GE's major internally grown business successes stemmed from outside the strategic planning system. Similarly, the more recent failure of Videotext, one of the most heavily researched business projects of recent years, shows that research and a sophisticated planning process are no panacea.

As John Sculley argues, planning major change takes artistry. Analysis, numbers and charts can be misleading. 'In planning Apple's future I prefer to talk about ideas and beliefs instead. How do my ideas jibe with where people think the industry is going? How do our beliefs differ from the analysis?'

Change-minded organizations set direction not detailed strategy. They realize that forecasting is full of surprises and that more relevant than planning is being well informed and ready to grab opportunities when they come their way, which is often. Another major difference between change-minded organizations and others is that strategy is not divorced from implementation. The two are built together, the strategy and beginning to make it happen. It is not planning in a vacuum, with someone dreaming up the future and other people then figuring out how to make it happen.

There are two main kinds of planned change:

- Strategic

- Operational.

Operational change is about making improvements, in the short or sometimes long term, based on rapid response and adaptation. It is day-to-day change with which all managers are familiar. Chance plays a big part in deciding what and when change can occur. This type of planned change is opportunity change. The scope for systematic planning is usually limited. For instance, when the stock market crashed in November 1987 this had been predicted for more than a year. The Australian Robert Holmes à Court, who made his name holding company shares until someone else needed them for a takeover bid, found his assets worth far less than he had originally paid for them. Whether he went broke or not was one of the questions that fascinated observers at the time. Though Holmes could afford the best investment and planning support available it did him little good because, even if it rightly predicted the crash, what counted more was the opportunism of acting at just the right moment.

Strategic change deals with large scale strategic alternatives. It is about major shifts in one or more of the main elements of any organization:

- Technical system – fitting resources to aims; fitting people to roles; measuring performance, staffing and development

- Political system – who gets to influence things; distribution and balance of power across groups; managing succession politics; reward systems

- Cultural system – aligning culture with mission and strategy; forming an organizational culture; managing rewards to shape the culture; selection of people to build or reinforce culture.

These ultimately decide an organization's market share, its ability to innovate, to develop, change and survive. You can think of these three main components of strategic change as strands of a rope, hard to see from a distance yet clear when you come up close. Handling planned strategic change takes account of all three systems that make up the organization (see Chapter 1 on Models).

Strategic planning is the point at which leaders enter, a new definition of the situation is made and a description of the future created which lifts the experiments of innovators from the periphery to centre stage. The activities of pioneers, mavericks, the 'product champions' and outsiders are given a new place in the sun, their ideas cease being irrelevant and become the way forward.

Formal planning systems contribute to major change, they seldom generate it. Breakthrough ideas stem from elsewhere, such as outside factors, special studies, ideas from existing developments, the drive and vision of inspired people who want to change the world. These ideas are incorporated into plans preserving the illusion that the planning process works. Detailed strategic plans are frequently after-thoughts cloaking emotions and intuitions with an aura of sober judgement. Creating the plan is often far more important than the plan itself. It is a way of clarifying 'where we want to be', and as such is concerned with direction.

Plans dealing with new methods, products, services, and structures are important, though not always for the reasons that people think. They are symbols, advertisements which attract investors, games used to test people's commitment to ideas and they are a justification for taking action. It is easy to be blinded by the planning process, seeing the creation of a plan as a substitute for action – the paralysis of analysis. Action not plans leads to management success.

The planning process is about sharing vision, expectations, understandings and information. Thus it is a communication tool which can contribute to people working together better. Most strategic plans are notable in retrospect for what they did not include and judged solely on their predictive powers they are usually dismal failures. Their merit is in helping managers to communicate to each other, to employees, to shareholders and others where the organization is heading.

The planners

Strategic change has so many different variables that it does not readily lend itself to quantitative techniques or even formal analysis. Strategic planning relying on extensive documentation and elaborate research is symbolized by the rise and fall of the corporate planner. In the 20-year period to the mid 1970s corporate planning promised managers a convincing way to create the future. Reports bulging with forecasts and indicators of performance were the rage.

Organizations vied to produce volumes of figures, policy statements and strategic goals. The producers of these imaginative documents worked in a financial and economic climate where they could virtually make their forecasts occur. But by the late 1970s and 80s the climate had changed, and it became apparent that the planners and forecasters were not so talented after all.

Enterprises which are deeply committed to long term formalized planning systems tend to react to outside events slowly because they are locked into expensively created predictions. People are loathe to say that the vision of the future is wrong.

Contrary to the commonly held notion of how managers should act, at the strategic level managerial leaders avoid elaborate packages of goals since this can:

- SUGGEST that the issue is closed for discussion or debate

- CUT people off from useful information

- FOCUS opposition

- CAUSE rigidity; fixed goals are hard to alter – people's egos are involved

- OFFER hostages to fortune

- DAMAGE security; good people may leave the organization taking secrets with them.

Box 13

Benefits of formal planning systems

- Push people periodically to look ahead

- Stimulate vigorous communications about goals, strategic issues and resource allocations

- Prompt longer term or more detailed analysis than would otherwise occur

- Lengthen time horizons and thus protect long term investments such as research and development

- Provide a psychological backdrop and information framework about the future against which short term decisions can be calibrated

- Fine-tune existing commitments

- Help implement strategic change once this has been decided upon

It is more accurate to see strategic planning as a series of smaller decisions made over time which evolve into major change. It may be hard to identify a single strategic plan that has momentous implications. For example, the decision by General Motors in America to produce smaller cars was not originally contained in a single plan. It came from a number of turning points.

So what use are formal planning systems? Their main contribution is providing support for making choices about how the future might look. They offer benefits such as those shown in Box 13. Even with formal planning, change is messy, involving an erratic path of learning and developing ideas.

Incrementalism versus the radical shift

The urgency faced by many major and medium-sized organizations to change in order to survive places a premium on fast, radical change. The idea of the transforming leader, the manager who inspires and shakes the entire organization, is a reflection of the pressures for change which exist throughout the industrial world.

An impatience to make things happen is increasingly reflected in the tenure of managers who seldom stay more than a few years in their job and hence need to produce results in a hurry. There is an apparent divide between those organizations and their leaders who see strategic planning as a constant process of staying flexible, visionary, and radical, and those where change is preferred as a more incremental, step-by-step process.

The split between the incremental approach and the transforming one is a false division. There are many elements of incrementalism which the rapidly changing organization must adopt. Similarly, those which rely on the incremental approach must often accept a large amount of change that from many viewpoints is radical.

Incrementalism has been called iterative and criticized as 'muddling through'. Yet this is how many of the world's most successful organizations operate. Strategic planning is not simply muddling through, nor is it an exercise of power or the use of formal planning systems:

> **Change strategies emerge from a series of sub systems**
> **which themselves may be highly rational. It is the**
> **total approach which is incremental.**

Sub systems may deal in a highly disciplined way with specific issues such as acquisitions, market diversifications, structural change, and so on. Or strategic planning can be focussed on important new organizational groupings such as in Pepsi Cola, where people are put in charge of managing 16-ounce returnable bottles, merchandising, convenience stores and so on. Cohesion arises from combining a rigorous approach with judgement, intuition and flair.

Despite criticisms of incrementalism as either too slow or muddled it can be: purposeful; effective; and proactive. Major organizational change is usually handled incrementally because strategic change has its own timing and driving forces. Managers need time to think through new roles, decide who can do what, assess individual reactions, develop solutions to new problems and so on.

Incrementalism is the essential thread that links:

- Information gathering

- Analysis

- Testing

- Behaviour

- Power considerations.

Unlike the preparation of a fine banquet it is impossible for even a visionary managerial leader to orchestrate all internal decisions, external environmental events, behaviour and power relationships, technical and information needs so that at any precise moment they join coherently.

By developing broad brush statements of the desired future incrementalism assists by making results realistic and attainable. Strategic plans are the springboard from which management action is launched. They do not simply come from managers' heads, but involve input and influence from people inside and beyond the immediate organization. There must normally be some sense of shared vision about the future around which detailed plans are constructed and actions agreed.

A road map

There is no system to guarantee strategic change. Planning mechanisms, project teams or sophisticated matrix structures all assume that the task is like drawing a correct wiring diagram. There may be no single solution because of conflicting interests within:

- The organizational hierarchy

- The different operational units of the organization.

With hierarchical structures, communications travel up and down usually without skipping levels, making it slow to develop plans and providing plenty of room for errors and misunderstandings about what is being attempted. With few operating levels and many autonomous units, it is hard to tie all the segments into a coherent strategy with a clear sense of direction.

Planning strategic change is like creating a road map of where you want to go, marking out the main routes, not compiling a manual of instructions for how to get there. It hardly matters whether the plan is accurate, it is more important that there is some attempt to visualize and influence the future. The three elements common to all planning approaches are:

- DIAGNOSIS – choosing the desired end state

- PLANNING – how to handle the transition state

- INTERVENTIONS – actions to move towards the end state.

(See Chart 2 in Chapter 1 on Models.)

Defining the future and how to get there is concerned with stating the fields of activity in which the organization is going to excel. Interventions are about implementation and it is this area of change management that until recently has been relatively neglected, often in favour of time spent on bureaucratic systems for deciding direction and devising strategy.

Deciding on the end state

In essence you are trying to answer the question:

If we succeed what will the final end state be like?

The end state describes in terms of a battle where the organization will be. For commercial concerns it is the battle to compete and win. For public and voluntary agencies it is the battle to offer service users maximum choice and quality of service.

Competitive strategies must enable the company to achieve strategic superiority. This is managed either through: occupying a distinct place in the market place via quality, image, distribution or innovation; or through achieving low production costs relative to competitors.

Public service strategies must enable the agency to be either highly responsive to user needs; or to use resources so cost effectively that a relative lack of flexibility is accepted.

In striving towards a new end state, organizations will implement their strategies so as to affect structures, policies, authority, tasks, styles, roles, and so on. Since organizations do not stop developing, it may not be obvious when the new state has been reached. Occasionally, when the end state is visualized in numerical terms, it is easier to decide the outcome. However, this is seldom motivating enough to sustain an organization through its many ups and downs on the way to the desired end state.

In order to define a vision of the end state some organizations use outside consultants while others use their formal planning system, and still others rely on leadership qualities. No matter how it is done there must be decisions about:

- How big a change are we talking about?
  How different will the end state be from the present one?

- How fast will we move towards the end state?
  A wrong choice about the time scale can threaten an organization's survival. Major change condensed into two to three years means that the period will be an unstable one; major change spread over three to five years means that during this time the organization will be in a transitional phase; finally, a major change spread over five or more years means that the organization is essentially always stable.

- What is the likely impact of the changes for achieving the end state?

In answering these questions managerial leaders will be moving towards defining a position in which the organization has a position of strategic excellence. Cuno Pumpin, Professor of Business Administration at St Gallen, one of the leading business schools of Europe, defines a strategic excellence position (SEP) as:

a capability which enables an organization to produce better than average results over the long term compared to its competitors.

Planning strategic change aims to identify and move the organization to occupy strategic excellence positions.

The SEP concept has assisted international companies such as Audi, Ciba, and Geigy. There are some basic rules which have major ramifications for planning change (see Box 14). They concentrate energy, thought, and ultimately resources – just as a magnifying glass focusses the sun until it creates a fire.

Box 14

Ten laws of strategic excellence positions

1　The existence of SEPs determine a company's success

2　SEPs are developed by the allocation of resources

3　The resources allocated to a given SEP must be withdrawn from other possible SEPs, unless there is synergy between them

4　The number of SEPs that can be developed is limited

5　Once an SEP has been developed it can be maintained only if it is constantly nurtured by the allocation of appropriate resources

6　SEPs may stand in a harmonious, neutral or conflicting relation to each other

7　Strong SEPs can only be developed if all the company's specialist managers are involved in inter-disciplinary co-operation

8　Developing SEPs is a medium to long term activity

9　The benefits of SEPs change over time

10　There is a close relation between a company's corporate culture and its SEPs

---

Source: The Essence of Corporate Strategy, C Pumpin, Gower Publishing, 1987

The transition state

A major difference between planned and operational change is the need to plan for the transition state. With opportunity change the impact of the transition stage may be relatively small. But for strategic change you need to:

- RECOGNIZE that the transition state is significantly different to the end state

- MAKE separate plans for handling it

- PAY particular attention to detecting blocks

- TOLERATE behaviour or action which reflect people's difficulty in adapting to new arrangements.

In 1984 the London Borough of Croydon decided that it needed a new direction for its services to adults. The aim was to create better services and also balance a steadily growing bias towards children's services absorbing a disproportionate share of resources.

To promote the change it wanted all existing services for adults to be concentrated into a single operational division. However, full implementation lasted nearly two years and the benefits did not appear for some time. Meanwhile existing services had to be maintained. At the start of the transitional period the senior management developed a phased plan for moving into the new structure, providing opportunities within work teams for discussion and communication about the changes. Managing the transition stage was more complex and stressful than the eventual end state.

Thus the transition state is a distinctly different one to the desired end state and may require its own separate plan of action. Because this interim stage is often turbulent and stressful, attention must be paid to how the plan is progressing and to detecting blocks to progress. Many sensible plans fail because of insufficient attention to what is happening during the transition phase.

Devising a strategy

Since there is no science of strategic change there are many views on how actually to achieve strategic shifts:

- Appeal to common sense

- Re-educate people

- Use power.

Common sense. This approach to strategic change relies on people being rational and acting sensibly, once they see their own self interest. Believing this you would concentrate on communicating the proposed changes clearly, showing the gains involved and assume that people will be sensible, motivated and follow your lead.

Re-education. This approach assumes that, even though the change you are planning is strategic, people will only understand it on a personal level in which what matters is how they see their world, their attitudes, values, skills and significant relationships. Knowledge and information are not enough. Believing this you would plan strategic change by helping people to understand and cope with their future through, for example, training, career development, job redesign, redefining roles and so on.

Use of power. This approach says that people with less power comply with the plans, direction and leadership of those with greater power. Believing this you would select actions which emphasize what people must do, when they are to do it and who ensures that they do it.

While change may stem from a mixture of all three approaches, managers tend consciously or unconsciously to subscribe to one rather than another. What view you hold determines your change strategy. Review to what extent you are biased too much in favour of one particular approach.

Regardless of your particular preference you will need to engage in a purposeful and politically astute process. The crudities of management by objectives or narrow goal setting are seldom enough. To devise a viable plan there are several elements to consider as shown in Box 15.

Box 15

The elements of strategic planning
• Sense needs
• Build awareness
• Broaden support
• Create commitments
• Focus developments
• Seek accountability
• Maintain the dynamic

Sense needs

Deciding on major organizational change requires the instinct of a blood hound, sniffing out areas where change is required. The evidence may be found in market research ratings, profit centres, the relationship between the organization and its distributors, in technological developments, in what teams say, in a stream of unexpected problems and so on. There are many formal tools for detecting where and when strategic change is needed, and though initially the targets will be vague and ill defined, gradually it becomes clearer what must be changed and how.

Vision plays a large part in sensing needs. Many organizations have been built on an unwavering vision of what the future would look like and what is needed. The power of that early vision can make market research, analysis and other planning techniques a distraction (see Chapter 16 on Sensing).

Build awareness

Demonstrating a need for major change is an essential part of evolving a strategy. There must be a level of common awareness in the organization that a major change is now required. For instance, at Pepsi Cola one time president John Sculley wanted to invest in larger regional groups of independent bottlers. However, most of the available resources were being siphoned off into the new fast food businesses and he concluded that there would be no general awareness of the need he had highlighted until these other businesses had succeeded.

Generating enough 'comfort' for the idea of strategic change may demand more than study groups, debates, seminars, surveys and so on. It will also need political skill in generating a will to listen to what may sometimes prove to be unpleasant or hard truths.

Broaden support

As awareness of the need for strategic change spreads, there are usually many informal discussions probing positions and challenging assumptions. At this stage it is essential not to lose patience with the sceptics and doubters. Adopting a new strategic direction challenges the *status quo* and many existing vested interests. There may be whole layers of people who find it easier to say no rather than yes, to pour cold water on ideas rather than encourage them.

The way forward is to seek constructive movement within the organization without initially threatening major power centres. For example, discuss proposals in principle with the promise that details will be re-presented. Goals remain broad and unrefined.

Create commitments

It is rare that everyone who matters in an organization agrees on the need for major change or how to achieve it. Create pockets of commitment to new directions, while projects are explored and options are kept open. This will mean being opportunistic about building small, isolated commitments into a more powerful force – to generate critical mass.

Focus developments

As the nature of the strategic goals crystallize, they must be channelled into specific proposals. For example, a crucial committee can help educate and neutralize opposition. At this stage goals begin to be quantified with outline timetables and costs. This is also the stage when marginal proposals are dropped.

Seek accountability

With the firming up of goals more people have to be made accountable for specific results. For example, it must be clear who does what, by when and with what resources. A useful way to clarify accountability is to state 'who owns' the responsibility for seeing that the plan becomes action.

Maintain the dynamic

Many strategic change efforts, after starting well, fizzle out. The art of strategic planning is to develop ways to maintain the momentum over a prolonged period which may stretch into years. Relying on many people to sustain the strategic change effort is better than relying on just a few individuals. Similarly, it may be sensible to pile change upon change so as to ensure the pressure behind the strategic shift is perpetuated. Also by having an 'owner' for ensuring that the plan happens there is an improved chance that the dynamic of change will be watched and if necessary action taken to maintain it.

GUIDELINES

- CLARIFY whether you are planning for strategic or operational change

- ACTION not plans lead to management success

- AVOID elaborate packages of goals

- BASE plans on a shared vision about the future

- USE the main elements of strategic planning as shown in Box 15

- OBTAIN constructive movement within the organization without initially threatening major power centres

- LEAVE goals broad and unrefined in the early stages of strategic planning

- CREATE pockets of commitment to new directions

- DETERMINE who 'owns' the responsibility for pursuing strategic change

- DEVELOP ways to sustain the momentum of the strategic change

- CLARIFY what the final end state will be like; how big a change we are talking about; and how different the end state will be from the present one

- MAKE separate plans for handling the transition state

- DECIDE how quickly the strategic change will occur.

Procedures
9. Action sequence

The staff were all anxious. The ailing UK retail concern Woolworths had been bought from its American parent by a new British board. Did the 1982 change disguise an asset stripping programme? Could the new team turn the ship around?

For years the company which was rich in assets and people had been poor on results and profits. The new management's main concern was to win staff support and gain commitment to a new strategy. To assess part of the problem an attitude survey was conducted amongst the 20,000 employees who nearly all replied. Their message was clear:

● Fear existed at all levels

● Management meant 'I tell, you do'

● Customers were seen as a threat

● Communications were generally poor

● Bureaucracy was rife.

Managers were treated like clerks, being conditioned to handle systems, procedures, stock and property. People were to be manipulated and disciplined. Creativity and initiative had neither been expected nor rewarded. The survey results indicated a heartfelt cry from all staff to return pride and confidence in working for Woolworths. Fundamental perceptions had to be changed about what it meant to manage people. The behaviour of a great many people had to be modified.

To get action the top management decided to send a signal across the company: management means doing things right, leadership means doing the right things (see also Chapter 2 on Leadership). All 1,200 managers were to be given training spread over three years. The first year would emphasize leadership and the team; the second leadership and the customer; and the third leadership and the business. The aim was to revitalize leadership skills, sharpen awareness of customers and improve managers' perceptions of the entire business, not just their own part of it.

As a result of trials the stores' management structure and how they looked inside were changed. There was more emphasis on personal responsibility, more scope for the development of teams and freer, more open communication. The overall results of Woolworths Holdings, bolstered by strategic takeovers, improved from a £6 million profit in 1982 to a spectacular £115 million in 1986–7.

Rejuvenating Woolworths was a classic case of major organizational change. It is possible to see in the process logical steps which are common to all large scale organizational change efforts. The main action steps are those shown in Box 16 (see also Chart 2, page 5).

Box 16

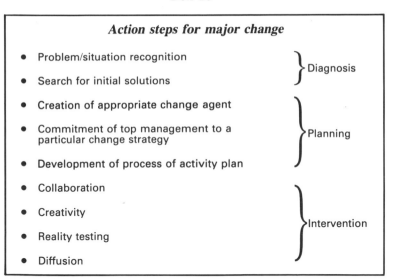

Action steps for major change

- Problem/situation recognition
- Search for initial solutions

} Diagnosis

- Creation of appropriate change agent
- Commitment of top management to a particular change strategy
- Development of process of activity plan

} Planning

- Collaboration
- Creativity
- Reality testing
- Diffusion

} Intervention

Problem/situation recognition

The start of handling change is to find out what needs doing. This involves scanning the environment, looking both inside and beyond the organization, diagnosing the type of change required, assessing the direction, rate and magnitude of change needed. From these investigations strategies are developed.

While often presented as a logical, systematic process it is far more an intuitive one. Systematic analysis highlights problems and situations; the more thorough the study, the longer the list of things to do. The managerial leadership task is to produce a list of priorities requiring intensive effort. Discovering what is happening and what must be done means leaving your desk and seeing for yourself. A study conducted by Professor Revans some years ago indicated that the most important issue for workers in several factories was the extent to which they felt that the management listened to them. Listening is a key skill at this stage (see also Chapters 15–20 on Techniques).

Simplify issues by focussing on one or two main problems rather than half a dozen or more (see also Chapter 5 on Simplification). Pick the fundamental and primary issues, not secondary concerns. Only by doing this can you create a momentum for a common view of the situation. Before action can be formulated convincingly most of the key people in the team or the organization must also hold this view. No matter how complicated the situation, the areas in which change will occur reduce to those shown in Box 17.

Box 17

The focus for change
• Impact on people • Decision process • External environment • Power groupings &   aims of policy makers } Political
• Structure • Technology & use of   techniques • Tasks being done • Regulatory systems } Technical
• Climate of the organization • Norms & values • Staff qualities } Cultural

As there is often a wide divergence in how priorities are perceived across the organization, it may be necessary to conduct goal setting exercises to identify new directions and specific targets for action. Goal setting exercises bring together key personnel who help list the issues within the overall problem statement and then work together to define ways of tackling them. Alternatively, the job may become one for a special project group reporting back to senior management.

Search for initial solutions

Faced with a complex situation requiring change a common management reaction is 'Where do I begin?' Successful change efforts suggest that change should start at those points in the system where some stress and strain exist, but not where these are the greatest. Strain causes dissatisfaction with the *status quo* and thus becomes a motivating factor for change in the system. Look carefully at the recipients of the proposed changes, to see if they can be grouped or segmented so as to benefit from slightly varying change strategies?

Stagnating organizations develop many layers of filters to keep out the external world. One solution may be to deliberately introduce conflict. This can stimulate the creation of mutual goals and values, integrating individuals into groups. Confrontation meetings, for example, can ensure that problems are aired along with alternative solutions.

Problems recognition narrows the task, putting crucial not marginal issues on the agenda for action. At this stage you are only looking for an outline of possible action and this must reflect:

- Available resources

- An acceptable time scale.

It is no use, for example, devising a major change programme which cannot be properly financed. Similarly, there is no point planning a major change programme lasting too long. The major strategic decision to decentralize the London Borough of Islington's services into two dozen local community centres had to be completed within three years, before the next local government elections.

At this early stage in the process of organizing the change effort you should also identify how much commitment to change exists. Woolworth's survey, for example, revealed that there was widespread staff support for it:

**The smaller the commitment, the more intense
the change effort required.**

Now is also the time to begin developing some criteria for judging the impact, the success or failure of any change. The short term criterion may well be profits for a commercial concern or a service offering more consumer choice in the case of a public agency. The longer term is represented by the vision which managerial leaders develop. There will be many indicators of performance available. For example, once Apple Computer had begun making profits again in 1986 the change targets selected for one year onwards were 50,000 MacIntosh sales a month, 50 per cent greater profit margins and a stock price of $50 a share. Some possible criteria for judging solutions are shown in Box 18.

Box 18

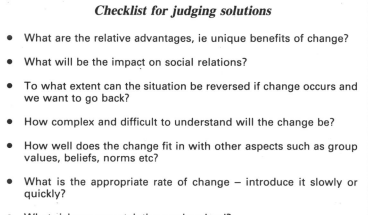

Checklist for judging solutions

- What are the relative advantages, ie unique benefits of change?

- What will be the impact on social relations?

- To what extent can the situation be reversed if change occurs and we want to go back?

- How complex and difficult to understand will the change be?

- How well does the change fit in with other aspects such as group values, beliefs, norms etc?

- What is the appropriate rate of change – introduce it slowly or quickly?

- What risks or uncertainties are involved?

- What commitment is required to implement and sustain change?

In formulating solutions it is also sensible to consider:

How secure is it to undertake change?

This means looking at how individuals are feeling and the organizational factors making it unsafe to tackle situations, such as perceived likely success or failure of change, confidence, self esteem, culture climate etc. Any major change has a ripple effect and cannot be neatly confined to one part of the enterprise. For example, to change behaviour at one level of a hierarchical organization it is necessary to achieve complementary and reinforcing changes both above and below this level. Reviewing safety and how people are feeling determines whether to phase in the changes or use the big bang approach.

As the Woolworth experience underlines, formulating a major

change demands attention to organizational norms. These are the hidden values influencing how change will be received and managed. If an organization has long held beliefs, traditions, and a history of minimal change, some formal process may be needed to unfreeze attitudes and behaviour. Woolworth's tackled this by creating an 'Excellence programme' for store staff which, in parallel to the leadership programme for managers, offered rewards, recognitions for achievement and progress towards a standard of personal and team achievement. Other ways of unfreezing attitudes also exist, such as confrontation meetings, project groups, education programmes, and so on.

A common mistake often made at this early stage in deciding how to handle change is to have a favourite idea about how to tackle the situation. For instance some managers always restructure, others always improve communications, others replace people and yet others focus on production and control systems. It is important to avoid being 'solution minded' and imposing ways of tackling situations which are not actually needed. A fear of being thought indecisive sometimes causes insufficient time and effort to be spent on reviewing the choices.

Another common mistake is thinking that management's main role is exhorting and selling the change. Advocating change, however, is no guarantee of movement. Similarly, although problem analysis may quickly reveal what needs doing, the next step is not necessarily to announce what will happen next. Many major changes can be achieved almost imperceptibly and can influence thinking throughout the enterprise without a big announcement. In fact, the Japanese often criticize Western managers for 'Announcementitis', that is rushing to make public statements about proposed solutions which creates resistance.

Create appropriate change agent

Change agents are the catalysts for making things happen, precipitating and often leading the change effort. They may be existing managers, project teams, a representative group charged with a task, a team of consultants from elsewhere in the organization, specialists recruited from outside, and sometimes the entire staff group.

Selecting a change agent is important to ensure that the change strategy happens. The responsibility for 'ownership' of the change effort must be identified as it will be hard to switch horses once the race for change has begun. Since major change may take years to implement there needs to be some continuity in ownership of the change effort. This is why a chairman, managing director or senior member of the managing board of an organization is often selected to lead the change.

A popular change agent in recent years has been the corporate entrepreneur or product champion. The latter has a high need for achievement and visibility and fights hard for a particular organizational change because they identify their own personal success with it. The change agent can thus be selected from a variety of different people or groups. What matters is choosing one that is appropriate to the change required and ensuring long term continuity.

Commitment to a particular change strategy

People will accept a general aim and argue endlessly about the specifics. At this stage the central issue is 'how will we manage the change?' not 'what objectives shall we set?' It is more important to have:

- A clear sense of direction

- A description of the desired end state after the change

- Full commitment by senior management to the proposed way of achieving the end state.

In order to gain senior management commitment it is better to have general goals, as opposed to highly specific, measurable or quantitative ones. These general goals help to promote cohesion; they make people feel comfortable with the idea of change; create identity and a sense of common well-being; and promote creative problem solving.

Managers responsible for achieving major change over a lengthy period may have difficulty in obtaining the backing of top management since it is often hard to demonstrate convincingly that the results are achievable, and are the best use of resources. For example, there may be pressure to put the resources to more immediate productive use, such as spending them on advertising, than investing in research and development. Unless top management are behind the broadly defined change programme and involved in seeing that it happens, the chances of a major change effort succeeding are much reduced. Many organizations that have launched programmes to improve the quality of their products with only token top management commitment have inevitably run out of steam.

Finally, commitment to the chosen change agent is also required. The latter must have ready access to top management to report and discuss how the change effort is going and whether further help is needed to keep it moving.

Develop process or activity plan

This stage converts 'How will we manage the process of change?' into a detailed map of the change effort. There are now more specific aims which can be broken down into a variety of detailed tasks to be performed. Since every organization is unique there can be no precise definition of an effective development process or activity plan, but the features of such a plan are suggested below.

A strategic plan which does not lead to action is not much use. It must also be sufficiently different from what has happened in the past to be setting a new direction. In judging its likely effectiveness people will expect to understand how one action relates to another. Thus, for example, in the Woolworth's training programme the company knew how the first year's programme led into the second and then into the third and how they all tied into a single overall aim.

An effective activity plan can be scheduled and the main staging posts identified without going into great detail . This means specifying who does what to whom by when. The use of networks and critical path techniques are sometimes helpful at this stage.

Any plan for handling major change must also be capable of being adapted to meet unexpected situations. The more detailed the aims the harder it will be to modify in new situations, so it is usually preferable to keep the plan simple and have a range of contingency plans which respond to some of the more important 'what if . . .' situations.

It is worth considering creating a separate plan for handling the transition state – those dynamic stages the organization will go through in order to reach the desired end state. Since the latter can be months or even years away there is often a need for temporary structures or arrangements. Most of the stresses arising from the change effort will certainly be in evidence during the transition state which therefore justifies a plan of its own if the change is a large one.

To steer the transition stage it may be sensible to create a separate structure, such as having a senior manager to handle and coordinate it; a project manager reporting to the board; the use of existing members of the hierarchy; a special group drawn from those sub sections of the organization that will be affected by the change; natural leaders; a representative sample from each part of the organization; reliable colleagues and so on.

Whoever handles the transition state must have authority to keep it moving, command the respect of top management and front line employees and possess good interpersonal skills. Whatever the temporary system, if it is to work well it must be properly communicated to everyone, and understood.

You cannot make a complete plan for change. There is no science of organization change and the more senior you are in the organization the more you will lack vital information which is held elsewhere and usually lower down in the organization. Focus on direction and keeping up the momentum of the plan.

Collaboration

Not every manager experienced in handling large scale change agrees on the importance of collaboration. Some believe in using management power to force change with or without support from those affected. Others feel that collaboration is essential if the change is to work properly. Studies of successful change efforts suggest that it pays to identify those sub systems primarily involved in the change and to build a commitment through participation in problem solving and discussion.

Commitment comes from genuinely seeking suggestions for action and using these where appropriate. To be seen as responsive to ideas you may need to encourage the involvement of people who appear opposed to the plans. The benefits of this are:

- Opponents often insert reality into management thinking about what is feasible

- Those outside formal decision centres often underestimate the difficulty of achieving change; by encouraging them to participate they will often become more realistic.

Collaboration sounds a vague idea, in practice it simply means working with those sub systems vital to the change effort to create a realistic plan (see also Chapter 4 on Commitment). Collaboration in making the planned change will occur when some or all of the conditions shown in Box 19 exist. (See also Chapter 11 on Participative Decision Making.)

Creativity

Planning and implementing change depends on creativity. As plans turn into more detailed tasks there is the opportunity and indeed

Box 19

Conditions for collaborating with planned change

- People feel pressure to change and participate in designing it

- Early changes bring tangible results and are limited in scope

- Change is spread throughout the organization, affecting many people and producing positive benefits in terms of attitudes

- People are helped to behave more effectively in solving problems and relating to each other

- There is an improved organizational performance

---

the need to question old ways and to acknowledge that they may no longer be effective. For many people the exciting and attractive aspect of change is that it introduces new ways of thinking, working and doing.

Whether in the shape of innovative new products or new groupings of resources, creativity offers scope for people to express their personality and skills.

The creativity for precipitating major organization change is sometimes crushed by the inertia of the old ways and existing commitments. Organizations have tried many approaches for releasing the creative energies that undoubtedly reside within the enterprise. Much depends on the prevailing culture and particularly leadership as to whether genuinely new ways of doing and thinking will emerge.

You can assess the climate for creativity in your own organization by examining how the so-called 'odd balls' are treated. These are the mavericks, the rebels and people who are often labelled as 'difficult'. The history of successful innovation and change is replete with how such individuals have seen what others have refused to see and against heavy odds have eventually been influential in forcing the necessary organization shifts.

Change brings the ideas of those on the periphery to the centre stage. Minority views, struggling projects, 'strange ideas' suddenly become respectable as the organization shifts direction. Thus during the change process the management task is to encourage creativity in new ways of thinking that will enable the change plans to work. For this to occur there must be a climate of tolerance for exploring new possibilities and for testing out previously dismissed ideas.

Reality testing

Many aspects of large scale organizational changes may first need testing on a small scale to see whether underlying ideas and solutions work. This is equivalent to test marketing a product in one part of the country before launching it nationally. Often top management decides that it simply has no time for this luxury and must risk the change without reality testing. It is, however, worth testing both the readiness and capability of sub systems to change. Launching a major change programme which assumes a general willingness to respond and then meets major resistance may delay for years the achievement of real change.

An obvious area where reality testing is sensible is when management is relying on training to produce important results. There needs to be some evidence that the proposed training plan will indeed contribute as expected to the change effort before it is used on a big scale involving many employees.

Diffusion

Diffusion is concerned with follow through – seeing that agreed and sometimes tested changes permeate the organization. This is one of the weakest areas of handling change and the one which is least well researched.

It is important for management to monitor whether the required changes are actually taking place and according to the agreed timetable. This follow-up is hard work and many managers find it the least creative and congenial of the steps required for producing major change. Lack of diffusion, caused by a failure to monitor, explains why perfectly sensible change plans sometimes fail (see Chapter 14 on Tracking).

GUIDELINES

- LOOK inside and beyond the organization to determine the change situation

- LISTEN to learn about changes needed

- USE goal setting exercises to help determine change requirements

- LIST priorities to focus intensive effort on change

- START the change effort where some stress and strain exist, not where these are the greatest

- CONSIDER creating mutual goals and values through introducing conflict

- MAKE action plans reflect available resources and an acceptable time scale

- DEVELOP criteria for judging the impact of planned change

- REVIEW how individuals are feeling and factors that may make it unsafe to tackle situations

- AVOID being solution minded

- BEWARE of 'announcementitis'

- DECIDE who 'owns' the responsibility for the change effort

- GAIN senior management commitment in the early stages of planned change by having general rather than highly specific goals

- SCHEDULE the planned changes to clarify who does what and when

- CONSIDER creating a separate plan for handling the transition state

- FOCUS on direction and keeping up the momentum of the plan

- BUILD commitment through participation in problem solving and discussion

- ASSESS the climate for creativity in your own organization by examining how the mavericks are treated

- PROMOTE tolerance for exploring new possibilities, for testing previously dismissed ideas

- TEST the readiness of sub systems to change and their capability of doing so.

Procedures
10. Experimenting

Groucho Marx took one of his brothers to an expensive country golf resort. Claiming to be a golf wizard the brother hit the first ball, smashing a car windscreen. The second broke a resort window. Groucho exited rapidly, without his funny walk.

Like Groucho's brother anyone who has used a golf club soon discovers that this particular device can have unpredictable results. Much the same discovery can be made in organizations – there are relatively few reliable levers of change. As with selecting a golf club, whatever change lever you choose is a matter of judgement and often you must be willing to accept unpredictable results.

Managers are surrounded by uncertainty and trends, such as those outlined in Chapter 1 on Models including:

- Exchange rates

- Cost of energy

- Outcome of mergers, demergers

- Foreign competition

- Technology

- Consumer tastes.

Not every aspect of a particular change effort will be unpredictable. For instance, it may be quite possible to anticipate that what you want to achieve will meet resistance. Or that the decision to cut your product price will produce a definite response from your competitors. Because making changes means living with a certain amount of uncertainty, this is sometimes used unjustifiably as an excuse for avoiding or delaying action.

The fact that the outcome from a particular change is uncertain is seldom an argument for doing absolutely nothing. It warrants a review of the scenarios that might arise if change is implemented.

Managerial leaders recognize that in many respects planned change is unpredictable. They therefore:

● REVIEW the different types of change actions which are available

● CONSIDER what aspects of the change can be predicted – what are the likely scenarios?

● TRACK the results of a change effort

● RESPOND quickly and flexibly to new and unpredicted events.

If you manage a number of subordinates, try to convey to them that their efforts to make things happen are supported, as long as reasonable efforts have been made to think about the likely consequences. For small scale change efforts, minimize the demand for documentation. Large scale change should always be documented in advance as this provides a way of taking a critical look at what is proposed and a baseline from which to judge how well or badly the change effort goes.

Both the unpredictable nature and the scale of change which you may be seeking must figure in your thinking. Chart 12 below summarizes the situation:

Chart 12

Effects and outcomes

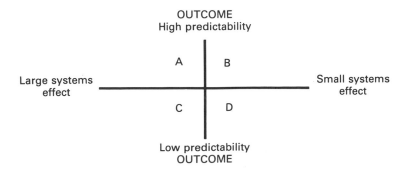

To achieve a major change you would normally prefer your selected change actions to be in sector A where the outcome is highly predictable. In reality, however, you may have to be reconciled to a high degree of uncertainty as in sector C. Even if you want a

relatively small change the outcome may still tally with sector D, ie hard to predict because you cannot be sure that the particular change lever will perform as expected. The search for certainty, or minimized uncertainty, is often a critical factor in deciding whether a particular change effort will succeed.

A particular change action may work for you yet fail dismally when tried by subordinates. For example, some managers love sending ticklers or 'reminders' that they are expecting some job to be done by a certain date. If this is part of their style it can produce results. Other managers, however, find that this approach does not seem effective when they try it and they have to resort to phone calls or personal visits to make something happen. Similarly some managers bent on major strategic change may rely heavily on market research or structural rearrangements, while others find that for them these are too slow and ineffective.

Experiments

Peer into a car mechanic's tool box and you will usually see dozens of different sized spanners. Watch the mechanic choose one. Often the first tool selected does not fit, and it is only by trial and error that the right one is located.

Like the mechanic, managers who want to make things happen must be prepared to experiment until they find the right lever of change that produces results. Working by trial and error (now sometimes called an iterative approach) is a relatively new approach for some organizations. The myth still exists that managers must always get it right first time and that organizations, particularly public bodies, cannot afford any mistakes.

Management science, with its emphasis on quantifying and rationality, has come to be regarded as almost a panacea for making organizations successful. Experiments on a large scale are therefore often condemned as irresponsible, too costly or a sign that not enough original research has been done to minimize uncertainty.

The man epitomizing this scientific approach to management was Robert McNamara who with his colleagues invaded the beleaguered Ford car corporation just after World War II. The Whiz Kids, as they were called, arrived as a package, selling themselves as a complete team to the company. They brought with them extraordinary skills of numeracy. Delving into every part of the crumbling car giant they asked endless questions. For a while they were dismissed as the Quiz kids.

The kids measured just about everything and the power of their information overwhelmed their critics. Their success in transforming Ford influenced several generations of managers, though the price has been high. Numbers and analysis have since dominated management thinking, particularly in some of the major international corporations, and the scope for experimentation has been drastically curtailed and sometimes virtually destroyed.

Gradually, managers around the world have begun to realize that quantifying, analysis and rationality have a built in conservative bias which values certainty above creativity and stifles change by tolerating only minimal experimentation. Aiming at near certainty frequently means banishing experiments and ultimately success.

A serious criticism of business schools has been that their graduates rely on the analytical approach, focussing mainly on short term goals with little recognition of the value of vision and long term investment. This kind of excessive rationality, which has characterized much of management thinking, has even infected organizations immune to the products of business schools. In Japan, for instance, a passion for numbers, order and quantifying has occasionally proved obstructive. For years the giant Nissan car firm was run by numbers-orientated finance experts who fiercely resisted the anguished pleas of committed employees, based in the States, to experiment with models adapted for the US market.

All the values of our culture seem to favour routine over creativity, the well established over novelty, the comfortable over the uncomfortable, boredom over excitement and precision over approximation. Managers are paid to be right and career prospects depend on avoiding mistakes. It is hardly surprising that experimentation and hence new products often stem from outside the industries and organizations which, logically, ought to be producing them.

Consumer product companies, for example, will often have a department or a specialist post devoted to new products. Since few managers want to put their name to a failure the result is endless idea generation, concept development, concept testing, market research and so on. But the new products never seem to reach the market. One top marketing expert asks his clients who are looking for a new product: 'How much are you prepared to lose?' If they cannot carry the loss of failure he argues that they cannot afford to go ahead with it.

Even failed experiments can teach something so that the next attempts have a greater chance of success. Unfortunately, finance-orientated directors and senior managers seldom see it that way. They are usually intolerant of failure, always demanding proof that success is a near certainty.

Because so many organizations suffer from an inability to handle experiments, there has been a search for ways to make them possible, despite the obstacles and organizational inertia. The most radical way has been the advent of the transforming leader who shakes the organization from top to bottom, revitalizing it with new vision and the courage to experiment (see Chapter 2 on Leadership).

Rather less grandiose, yet in some ways just as radical, is the idea of the Product Champion who pushes for a particular development within an organization. This person is expected to thrust past organizational constraints and be willing to experiment. Product champions generally identify themselves; the problem for organizations is how to help them succeed. A product champion will often try numerous new ways to bring about change in the search for something that works. This experimental learning approach makes them highly vulnerable:

● Look what he's cost us!

● His idea was crazy anyway

● She should never have been allowed to try it

● Who needs failures?

● I knew that it wouldn't work.

Of the many lessons to learn about using product champions to foster experimentation and hence change, probably the most important is:

**Don't let a product champion go down with
the product or idea.**

Product champions who have put their careers on the line in order to experiment with change must be rewarded not punished, recognized not given the cold shoulder. Less radical, yet still highly effective, is the approach epitomized by the 3M company 'to make a little, sell a little, make a little more' – in other words being willing to create a host of experiments and, if they show signs of succeeding, to back them further.

Having dozens of experiments happening simultaneously has several obvious advantages. First, the chances of a winning idea is increased simply by the law of averages. Secondly, by having so many experiments at once, it is harder for those who resist change to block them all. Some slip through unopposed or with only token resistance.

Studies of highly successful companies show that major change often arises from one or more people sneaking off and experimenting, often without official sanction. In the case of new products this may mean using scrounged materials, overtime and goodwill from colleagues. Meanwhile the megabucks are being spent elsewhere. Time and again these major plans hit obstacles or lose credibility and, like the Fifth Cavalry, up pop the more modest experiments to save the day.

Thus, an important contribution to promoting change is assisting these low level, often unofficial experiments. If you cannot actively fund them, then at least turn a blind eye to people doing them.

Whether the experiments concern people, products or cash, the results are unpredictable. Failure is always possible. Too often organizations have a culture of punishment for failed experiments. Punishment may be reflected in damage to one's career or some other unpleasant response, such as criticism or disciplinary action. Rules, procedures and tight controls tend to be developed as managers legislate against experiments which could fail. In these circumstances, only the brave or the foolhardy stick their necks out and attempt new ways of achieving better results.

Long term strategic change cannot flourish in a culture that punishes failed experiments, and this is why few really new organizational thrusts occur. Gradually, the organization becomes rigid and slow in its responses, unable to take advantage of new opportunities.

The language of experimentation is easy to recognize. People can be heard saying things like:

- Let's try it!

- Why don't we test it out?

- What will happen if . . . ?

- If we do that, how would we know whether it succeeds or fails?

- If it doesn't work we'll try something else

- Here's one way of finding out

- What do our customers think?

- We tried it and found . . . .

Equally you can tell when the climate is unfavourable to strategic change. People say things like:

- Too risky

- It could go really wrong

- We can't afford to learn by trial and error

- What counts is success

- You'd better be right

- You're ignoring the procedures

- Go ahead, but if it goes wrong you're on your own

- If we do that we'll tip off the opposition.

The last of these is a familiar catechism of some companies who reject experiments in the market place because they fear that this will alert their competitors. In practice, the failure to experiment is a worse fault, cutting them off from customers and learning how to meet market needs. What drives many experiments forward is the customer. Getting close to the customer will often provide a vital force for trying something new.

GUIDELINES

- CONSIDER what results of planned change can be broadly predicted – what are the likely scenarios?

- EXPERIMENT with different change actions till you get results

- AVOID the paralysis of analysis

- ATTENTION to organizational values and culture encourage an experimental approach

- MINIMIZE documentation for small scale change efforts

- FAVOUR creativity over routine

- WELCOME the failed experiment as a chance to learn

- DON'T let a product champion go down with the product or idea

- TRY out lots of ideas. Sheer quantity will often produce a winner

- LISTEN for and speak the language of experimentation

- GET closer to the customer to generate more experiments.

Procedures
11. Participative decision making

United Technologies is an American high technology company based in New England. It makes many different products, including recently the world's largest escalator at Hong Kong Harbour.

When Robert Daniell took charge in the mid 1980s his priority was to alter the management style. He let it be known that participative management was his way of doing things and he quickly involved senior managers in this approach.

Daniell wanted to reach beyond conventional training or development and 'open the eyes of our managers to the potential of participative management'. UT's new leader felt that the company was failing to use the tremendous reserves of energy and creativity of its employees. Managers controlled, they did not facilitate.

Changing the *status quo* usually requires support. Participation can help to obtain that support. In UT a key to promoting participative management was: 'empowering others and gaining support in the organization'.

International studies show that the more participatory the firm the greater its financial and other types of success. This is especially so when introducing new technology. What happened when New Scotland Yard, the London police headquarters, installed a huge Command and Control Complex is an example of linking technology decisions with participation.

The Complex changed jobs and working practices for both uniformed and civilian staff. Sophisticated equipment had to be installed and old skills replaced by new ones. An authoritarian approach to such a major change would have back-fired, leading to inefficiency and low morale.

Staff from many departments and all levels joined teams to find solutions to a mass of problems. These ranged from the design and layout of the equipment, and where it was to be installed, to the best type of chair for seating comfortably a 6-foot, 16-stone policeman or a rather lighter 5-feet-4-inch police woman.

Care was taken to involve staff fully in decision making. The team leading the changes marked the dimensions of the real loca-

114

tion at New Scotland Yard on the floor of an empty warehouse. Templates and mock-ups were moved about into different shapes, then tested for suitability. Criticism and suggestions were encouraged with a free interchange of ideas and comments. Where possible the team searched for consensus.

The result is a smooth running complex in which police and civilians enjoy a quiet, unstressed atmosphere with each operator working efficiently. Participation has clearly paid off. According to the British government's Work Research Unit greater involvement of employees in managing change and decisions helps organizations become more:

- PROFITABLE – through improved quality and lower unit costs

- ABLE to use their human resources

- ROBUST

- ADAPTABLE

- VIABLE in the long term

- CREATIVE

- EFFECTIVE and quicker at making changes.

When employees are involved better decisions are reached with more commitment to making them work.

Nailing down participation

Participation occurs when people are involved and influence decisions which are likely to affect them. At one extreme, zero participation means that employees do as they are told. At the other extreme, total delegated authority ensures that employees have the final say. Participation happens only between these extremes. It does not happen when there is either total management control or total worker control.

Participative decision making expands the influence in the organization of those who are lower down the hierarchy and affected by decisions. The two routes for achieving this are via:

- INDUSTRIAL DEMOCRACY – collective bargaining, through representatives

- PARTICIPATIVE MANAGEMENT – informal sharing of decision making at the work place, involving individuals.

The most widespread form of participation is the formal process by which employers and trade unions negotiate agreements. Highly structured and frequently bureaucratic, it often raises false expectations about the extent to which employees will be involved. A disillusioned employers' association in Sweden called it 'a gigantic apparatus for the creation of dissatisfaction'. Despite this, industrial democracy can lead to useful involvement in decisions and joint problem solving.

Participative management is an informal process. It relies on affecting people's behaviour not through constitutions but by managers talking directly with those who will be affected by the decisions. The two approaches thus take a different view on who will be involved. Formal systems focus on representatives, informal ones on individuals. Hence participation methods differ, as follows:

INDIVIDUAL	REPRESENTATIVE
Briefing groups	Collective bargaining
Attitude surveys	Joint consultation
Problem solving groups	Works council
Job enrichment	Worker directors
Autonomous work groups	Staff committees

These two approaches are not mutually exclusive, however. Participative decision making usually fails when managers rely on only one of the two approaches. Both are needed if the pattern of organizational decision making is going to be successfully altered.

Exclusive reliance on one or other approach leads employees to see participative decision making as manipulative and a ploy to remove resistance.

The ingredients

The above clarifies what we mean by participative decision making and some of the benefits. There are also several important ingredients to participative decision making, such as:

- Individual autonomy

- Group responsibility

- Organization-wide influence

- The nature of the decision making process.

Individual autonomy
Enhancing individual autonomy in organizations is increasingly recognized as a key for obtaining employee commitment to change. The Computer Management Group, for instance, which operates in the UK, the Netherlands and Germany with a staff of more than a thousand, has a written philosophy that begins:

> CMG is a successful company where each person is his or her own boss to the maximum possible extent.

Once people have achieved some of the more basic survival requirements in life they seek opportunities for self expression, satisfaction in what they do and an ability to arrange their own work lives as far as possible.

Giving people more autonomy or control over their lives does not lead to anarchy, it fosters responsibility and accountability. These make it easier to confront change, promote innovation and tackle inertia.

Group responsibility
Individual employees are usually part of a team or local work group. The latter is part of a larger group, department, division, subsidiary and so on. Both individuals and groups have a responsibility to the organization. Sometimes the groups' needs override those of individuals and occasionally *vice versa*. Participative decision making recognizes this fact by encouraging groups to take responsibility for their own actions. Individuals must exercise autonomy both within and outside the group.

Participative decision making provides a spur to groups becoming committed to change.

Organization-wide influence
Once you start trusting people to take part in the decision making process the effect is like a stone dropped into a pool of water, with ripples spreading throughout the enterprise.

Managers in both United Technologies and New Scotland Yard

obtained better results by letting many people have a direct influence on the decision making process. They realized that when both individuals and groups exercise their autonomy the benefits extend across the organization.

The decision process

The decision making process is shown in Chart 13. Several thousand managers and supervisors have confirmed that the nine-step process reflects what happens when organizations make choices.

If you want to promote participative decision making there are three useful check questions which can be applied anywhere along the paths shown in the chart:

- TYPE – what sort of decision is open to participation?

- STAGES – where in the decision making process will participation occur?

- EXTENT – how far will participation go, who will be involved?

Type

Not every decision is suitable for participation. For instance, if you are introducing short time working, redundancy and closure it will almost certainly fail.

Even if everyone is fully committed the scope for participation varies according to the type of decision, as shown in Box 20. The management task is to creatively seek ways to expand opportunities for participation, where appropriate.

Stages

The nine-stage process shown in Chart 13 is a useful aid for clarifying where participation will be possible and managerially acceptable. While the eighth stage of selecting alternatives is perhaps the most important, it is often mistaken for the entire decision process. Uncertainty about where participation is desirable may cause decision making to become diffuse, a slow, creeping consensus. This happened during the early 1980s when the Philips electrical group relied heavily on achieving participation and consensus in the eighth choice stage. This not only maintained the *status quo*, it also prevented responsibility from being clearly located. A major shake up in the second half of the decade shifted the balance towards participation in the other stages with key managers taking responsibility for making final choices.

Chart 13

The nine-phase decision making process

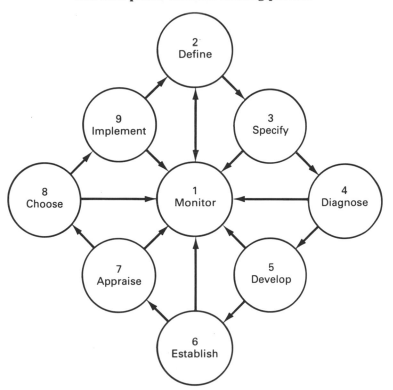

1 *Monitor* the environment constantly

2 *Define* the decision-problem or situation. In other words state precisely the boundaries

3 *Specify* the decision objectives. Clarify what you expect to achieve; define the risks and constraints

4 *Diagnose* the problem or situation and analyse causes

5 *Develop* alternative courses of action or solutions

6 *Establish* the methodology or criteria for appraising alternatives

7 *Appraise* alternative solutions or courses of action

8 *Choose* the best alternative solution or course of action

9 *Implement* the best alternative solution or course of action

Source: 'How to make a business decision, an analysis of theory and practice.', Archer ER. *Management Review*, February 1980, p58. Printed with the permission of the publisher, copyright 1980 by A Macom, a division of American Management Associations. All rights reserved

Box 20

Decision bands	
Decision band	Scope
BAND E	Policy making
BAND D	Programming – broad planning of execution of policy
BAND C	Interpretive – specific action decisions from range of options
BAND B	Routine – choice of how to do what is already specified
BAND A	Automatic – choice of operations within set process
BAND O	Vegetative – minimal discretion

Extent

How much participation will there be? While it can occur in any of the nine decision stages, the extent may vary, as shown in Box 21. Participation does not mean that everybody makes the decision or that there must always be consensus. For instance, a chemical firm that was highly committed to participative decision making involved all its employees in considering how it should spend £2 million pounds on further research. Many people shared in analysing opportunities, developing different courses of action, appraising alternatives and so on. Everyone was also aware that the ultimate choice of a course of action – the actual decision point – was reserved for the board of directors.

Similarly, in developing its participative management style the Formica Company, a leading producer of decorative laminates, identified these constraints:

**No loss of control of strategic decisions
at senior management level**

**No reduction in individual responsibility
as a result of participation.**

Box 21

Participation process gauge		
A	Management makes a decision without any discussion with employees. Employees are not informed of the decision afterwards	ZERO
B	Management makes a decision without any prior discussion with employees, and simply informs them of it afterwards	INFORMATION (one-way)
C	Management makes a decision without prior discussion with employees, and afterwards informs them of it and explains the reasons behind the decisions	INFORMATION bordering on COMMUNICATION (two-way)
D	Management sorts out its ideas, makes a plan, asks employees for their views, but tells them that because of other constraints their views can make little or no difference to the decision itself	COMMUNICATION bordering on CONSULTATION
E	Management sorts out its ideas, makes a plan, asks employees for their views, and fully takes them into account in making the final decision	CONSULTATION
F	Management fully shares the problem with employees without any preconceived plan – but after all the talking management makes the decision	CONSULTATION bordering on DECISION BY AGREEMENT
G	Management fully shares the problem without any preconceived plan – and after all the talking a decision is agreed	DECISION BY AGREEMENT
H	Management identifies the problem and asks employees to find and implement a solution	DELEGATED AUTHORITY

Source: Adapted from *Industrial Participation* by D Wallace Bell, Pitman, 1979

Participation appears to have the effect of increasing the control exercised by employees without decreasing that of managers. In more participative companies managers generally report feeling that they exercise more influence than managers in less participative companies. This is not only reassuring but also points to another myth about participation, namely that power is a fixed quantity – if someone gains it then someone else must lose it. The reality is that everyone's power can be increased by effective participative decision making (see also Chapter 6 on Power).

Real participation does not eliminate control, it only changes its quality.

Who wants it?

Do employees actually want to participate? In decisions about their own immediate work situation the answer is certainly yes. In middle and top management decisions the answer is less sure, varying in different organizational and national cultures.

Employees are modest in their expectations. They are more likely to care about issues that impinge on their daily lives than they are about more distant topics such as how profits are distributed, whether the organization should invest in bio-engineering and so on.

Lack of enthusiasm to participate in higher level decisions may be due, though, to an unhelpful participation process. For instance, employees may conclude that on some issues they lack expertise. Unless the gap between subordinates and superiors is reduced, attempts at participation merely increase mistrust. Participation schemes that have been imposed (whether by politicians, trade union leaders or management) without being designed to meet the particular needs of the work force are destined to failure.

A requisite of any system is that those involved should themselves have a say in the 'why', 'what', 'when' and 'how' of the system that is seen to be good for them. There should be a slow building of the awareness of shared goals, not an assumption that participation will automatically create a sense of common interest.

A decision aid

Of the various decision steps described in Chart 13 perhaps the most crucial is selecting the best alternative solution or course of action. Participation in this vital stage is seldom shared with more than a dozen people and often far fewer.

A practical and enjoyable way of clarifying what must be decided and how much participation will be encouraged is now possible using a personal computer. The Priority Decision System (PDS), for example, was developed at Brunel University and has operated in actual work situations for several years. It can be used by a single manager or a whole team and can potentially involve many people in situations where choices must be made.

Organizations such as ICI, British Telecom, Essex County

Council, IBM, Kodak, Lucas Aerospace, Shell and even the Cabinet Office have all used PDS. You need no knowledge of computers since everything is presented in straightforward English with clear instructions.

The first step in using PDS is to list the choices being considered. For example, a management team which must decide what projects to fund in the new financial year simply lists these in any order it chooses.

Next you name the people who will be involved in making the actual decision. Some of these will have much less authority or power than others. Participative decision making often fails because this uncertainty is never resolved.

PDS uses various methods to help decide how much influence each decision maker will be given. We can see it working in practice in a notional company headed by managing director Brian Smith. The board, consisting of the MD and four other directors, has to make a decision about which of seven possible projects it will back for further development.

The example in Box 22 shows the results of the board using PDS. The managing director has emerged with more influence than any other member of the board (26 per cent) without having more influence than his combined colleagues.

Box 22

Influence of decision makers (using the Priority Decision System)		
PROBLEM NAME: DM CRITERION USED: ALL THINGS CONSIDERED METHOD USED: SCALING		
RANK	DECISION-MAKER	INFLUENCE
1	A) MD: Brian Smith	0.261 (26.1%)
2	B) Director: P Jones	0.217 (21.7%)
2	D) Director: M White	0.217 (21.7%)
3	C) Director: L Brown	0.174 (17.4%)
4	E) Director: H Black	0.130 (13.0%)
	ALL DECISION-MAKERS	1.000 (100.0%)

The benefits of this approach are considerable. For instance, if managing director Smith asserts that he is merely 'first among equals' he would have to demonstrate this by being allocated an equal weight amongst all the other decision makers. Alternatively, as the most senior member of the team, he may expect to have more authority over a particular decision than his colleagues. Yet will his influence be sufficient to overrule everyone else? If so, what is the point of pretending that the members are participating? They are merely being consulted.

The results of two of the board members using PDS are shown in Box 23. Directors White and Black do not entirely agree on how the projects should be ranked. Both selected Project 1 as the most important, giving different rankings to the others. When all the board members have used PDS their views are combined to produce a team result as shown in Box 24. Project 1 emerges as a winner. Even allowing for the differences between the individual members of the board the computer system finds a high degree of agreement about the rankings.

Box 23

How two members of the Board rated the seven projects		
PROBLEM NAME:	DM	
CRITERION USED:	ALL THINGS CONSIDERED	
METHOD USED:	MAGNITUDE ESTIMATION	
DECISION-MAKER:	D) Director: M White	

RANK	OPTION	PRIORITY
1	A) PROJECT 1	0.180 (18.0%)
1	D) PROJECT 4	0.180 (18.0%)
2	C) PROJECT 3	0.157 (15.7%)
2	G) PROJECT 7	0.157 (15.7%)
3	E) PROJECT 5	0.135 (13.5%)
4	F) PROJECT 6	0.112 (11.2%)
5	B) PROJECT 2	0.079 (7.9%)
	ALL OPTIONS	1.000 (100.0%)

PROBLEM NAME:	DM	
CRITERION USED:	ALL THINGS CONSIDERED	
METHOD USED:	MAGNITUDE ESTIMATION	
DECISION-MAKER:	E) Director: H Black	

RANK	OPTION	PRIORITY
1	A) PROJECT 1	0.208 (20.8%)
2	C) PROJECT 3	0.182 (18.2%)
3	F) PROJECT 6	0.156 (15.6%)
3	D) PROJECT 4	0.156 (15.6%)
4	E) PROJECT 5	0.130 (13.0%)
5	B) PROJECT 2	0.091 (9.1%)
6	G) PROJECT 7	0.078 (7.8%)
	ALL OPTIONS	1.000 (100.0%)

Box 24

How the board ranked the projects		
PROBLEM NAME:	DM	
CRITERION USED:	ALL THINGS CONSIDERED	
METHOD USED:	MAGNITUDE ESTIMATION	
DECISION-MAKER:	TEAM	

RANK	OPTION	PRIORITY
1	A) PROJECT 1	0.241 (24.1%)
2	C) PROJECT 3	0.181 (18.1%)
3	D) PROJECT 4	0.155 (15.5%)
4	B) PROJECT 2	0.125 (12.5%)
5	E) PROJECT 5	0.122 (12.2%)
6	F) PROJECT 6	0.089 (8.9%)
7	G) PROJECT 7	0.086 (8.6%)
	ALL OPTIONS	1.000 (100.0%)

AGREEMENT MEASURE: 924
DECISION STANDARD: High degree of agreement between the team members

Seems complicated? Only in describing it. In practice the system rapidly reports on the decision making. What takes the time is collecting the information and feeding it into the computer. Even this can be shortened by letting people type in their choices.

Any number of people can participate in the Priority Decision System, although if the numbers exceed 20 it is necessary to do the decision making in batches.

With greater clarity about who is taking part in the decision and their degree of influence there is usually greater acceptance of the final result. There is less argument about why a particular course of action has been chosen and more sense of 'ownership' about the final decision. Maurice Hawker, a local government director in Essex, is blunt about the advantages: 'in place of watery compromises from four meetings, we get a valid consensus in 40 minutes'.

IPA

In Britain you can obtain help and advice about participative decision making from the Industrial Participation Association. This is an independent, voluntary grouping of individuals and organizations spread across most sectors of industry, commerce, public corporations, educational bodies and so on.

The IPA promotes employee involvement and its Code of Practice, issued jointly with the Institute of Personnel Management, has been recognized as providing a national framework for the most practical approach to participation in the UK. It has a small full time staff and offers various ways of helping people put participation into practice.

You can contact the IPA at 85 Tooley Street, London SE1 2QZ.

GUIDELINES

- DETERMINE people's expectations about and desire for participation

- START small. People need to get used to participative decision making

- AVOID top heavy consultative structures

- USE both formal and informal approaches to participation

- DECIDE whether to link implementation of participation with pressing problems being experienced by the organization

- CLARIFY the issues for which participation is needed

- IDENTIFY who is likely to be affected by a decision

- ENSURE that all parties with power participate

- EXPLAIN where in the decision process participation will be permitted

- DISTINGUISH between consulting and participation

- COMMUNICATE what is non-negotiable, where participation will not occur

- CREATE a credible timetable in which participation can occur

- CONVEY how people can participate – the mechanisms

- HELP people understand complex issues

- ENHANCE individual autonomy to gain employee commitment to change

- PROVIDE feedback on how the input from participation has been used

- MODEL a participative style, don't just exhort

- LOOK for system-wide effects of participative decision making

- ALLOCATE sufficient resources for the scheme including training and follow up

- ASSUME that participation will take a long time to become totally effective.

Procedures
12. Stress

Underpaid? Feeling unenthusiastic about your job? Unwilling to sacrifice family and social life? Working over 50 hours a week and harder than a few years ago? If this describes you then, according to a survey in the late 1980s by the London Business School, you are a typical manager!

In Britain and elsewhere managers are experiencing unprecedented changes in their working lives. Recession or sudden shifts in the economy reduce promotion opportunities, increasing the numbers of people stranded on a plateau in their careers.

Leaner corporate structures are making managers more accountable for profits, costs and results. Widespread use of information technology is eliminating the need for many middle managers. New technical skills are being demanded. No wonder occupational psychologists report increased stress at work from:

- The management role

- Interpersonal relations

- Organizational structure and climate

- Career prospects

- The work and home interface.

The causes and effects of stress are broadly summarized in Chart 14. A limited amount of stress is healthy, being the body's way of protecting us from potential dangers. It produces extra adrenalin which in turn stimulates greater energy and strength. As we breathe faster more oxygen is carried into the bloodstream and the inward surge of blood affects muscles and vital organs. We all have some degree of tolerance to stress, some greater than others. It is excess or chronic stress that is damaging. At some point managers show tension, fatigue and irritability which leads to emotional detachment, withdrawal, cynicism and rigidity.

Chart 14

Causes and effects of stress

CAUSES

Critical family and other non-work events	Individual characteristics	Work organization and tasks	Organizational change features

STRESS

Effects on individuals	Effects on work behaviour	Effects on organizational effectiveness

EFFECTS

Source: Work Research Unit.

A British study in the early 1980s found that the commonest stress symptom amongst women managers was tiredness. For junior and middle female managers depression came next, whereas for senior managers anxiety was rated as the second most serious stress symptom. Irritability and sleep troubles were also common.

How stress affects you will depend on whether you are flexible or inflexible, introverted or extroverted and how well you fit into your job. Signs that something is wrong include job dissatisfaction, job tensions, low sense of personal achievement, high rates of smoking, blood pressure, cholesterol or heart rate, and low self esteem.

Not all employers recognize that change is one of the most significant cause of stress. In late 1987, for instance, the BBC was publicly criticized by its own chief medical officer, Dr Ann Fingret, over its handling of an announcement of radical changes to radio services. Dr Fingret found that BBC employees were suffering unnecessary stress from waiting six months to learn if their jobs were to be axed under the five-year plan. The BBC medical adviser urged employers to develop more sensitive methods of easing their staff through periods of potentially stressful changes.

The impact of change on mental and physical health can have a disruptive influence on individuals and on the real cost to the organization, on whom many people depend. That cost is seldom considered either in human or financial terms. In handling change you need to be aware of the impact from stress:

On you

On others.

Impact on you

Proactive managers may experience tensions from trying to make things happen. It is hard being an effective change agent working long hours, and general 'overload' can soon lead to break-down. You need to retain a balance between commitment to the change objectives and commitment to your own health and perhaps your family's.

In the search for change you may find yourself going outside your own immediate role, for example managing project groups crossing organizational boundaries. There is considerable evidence that role ambiguity and role conflict can lead to lower job satisfaction, higher job related tension, greater feelings of futility and lower self confidence.

You could find yourself caught between two groups of people who demand from you different kinds of behaviour or functions. For instance, in pressing for change you may be meeting the expectations of some senior managers while running counter to others'. The greater the power of those sending conflicting role messages, the more the conflict produces job dissatisfaction and stress.

The impact of stress also depends on whether you are responsible mainly for people or for things. Responsibility for people usually means interacting with others, attending meetings, and working alone. Responsibility for people is significantly related to heavy smoking, raised blood pressure and so on. People who are mainly concerned with things, on the other hand, tend to be rather less affected by stress.

How you are affected by stress is closely related to whether you are a Type A or a Type B person. A Type A person is extremely competitive, strives for achievement and may be aggressive, hasty, impatient, restless, very alert, explosive of speech, with tense facial muscles, and feel under pressure of time and the challenge of responsibility. If you recognize something of yourself in this description you are also probably deeply involved and committed to your work, often to the relative neglect of other aspects of your life.

By contrast, Type B people tend to be more easy going, take difficulties in their stride, spend time on what they do, maintaining a careful balance between events and actions demanding their energy. A Type A person is more likely to suffer heart disease than a Type B person. Evidence has been accumulating that Type A people seem less interested in exercise and that their general lifestyle leads to ill health.

There are various ways of ascertaining your own stress level at any particular moment so that you can take counter measures. For example, check Box 25 for your chances of becoming ill due to stress in the next 12 months.

People preoccupied with either responding to or generating change often neglect simple health rules like taking a break for

Box 25

The stress 'league table'

(For anyone scoring more than 300, a major illness can be predicted within one year for 80 per cent of individuals. All life events within the past two years qualify.)

Death of spouse 100	Trouble with in-laws 29
Divorce 73	Outstanding personal
Marital separation 65	achievement 28
Jail term 63	Wife begins or stops work ... 26
Death of close relative 63	Begin or end school 26
Personal injury or illness 53	Change in living condition ... 25
Marriage 50	Revision of personal
Dismissal 47	habits 24
Marital reconciliation 45	Trouble with boss 23
Retirement 45	Change in work hours
Change in health of relative . 44	or conditions 20
Pregnancy 40	Change in residence 20
Sex difficulties 39	Change in school 20
Gain of new family member . 39	Change in recreation 19
Business readjustment 39	Change in religious
Change in financial status 38	activities 19
Death of close friend 37	Change in social activities 18
Change of job 36	Mortgage or loan less
Change in number of	than £8,000 17
arguments with spouse 35	Change in sleeping habits 16
Mortgage over £8,000 31	Change in number of family
Foreclosure of mortgage 30	get-togethers 15
Change in responsibilities	Change in eating habits 15
at work 29	Vacation 15
Son or daughter leaving	Christmas 12
home 29	Minor violation of the law 11

Box 26

Self-assessment exercise on nutrition

Choose the most appropriate answer for each of the statements below and place the letter of your choice in the space to the left.

1 I usually eat pastries or other foods high in quick energy as my only lunch:
(a) 2 times a week or fewer
(b) 3–4
(c) 5–6
(d) Every day

2 I drink _____ cola beverages (12 oz portion) per day:
(a) 2 or fewer
(b) 3–4
(c) 5–6
(d) 7 or more

3 I drink at least _____ cups of coffee or tea per day (excluding herbal tea):
(a) 2 or fewer
(b) 3–4
(c) 5–6
(d) 7 or more

4 I use _____ teaspoons of refined sugar per day:
(a) 4 or fewer
(b) 5–8
(c) 9–15
(d) 16 or more

5 I add salt to my food at meals (total shakes of a table salt shaker):
(a) 10 or fewer
(b) 11–20
(c) 21–30
(d) 31 or more

6 I eat chocolate (average-sized bar 1 oz):
(a) 1 bar or fewer a day
(b) 2–3 bars a day
(c) 4–5 bars a day
(d) 6 or more bars a day

7 I eat a doughnut or pastry as my only breakfast food other than a beverage:
(a) 2 times a week or fewer
(b) 3–4
(c) 5–6
(d) Every day

8 I smoke tobacco:
(a) Never
(b) Less than 1 pack/day
(c) 1–2 packs
(d) More than 2

9 I am exposed to the sidestream smoke of others around me:
(a) Not at all
(b) Less than 1 hr/day
(c) 2–4 hrs/day
(d) More

10 When I am around even minimal cigarette or cigar smoking my eyes or nose become irritated:
(a) Never true
(b) Seldom true
(c) Often true
(d) Always true

Score: [   ]

Scoring: a=1, b=2, c=3, d=4

A total score of 30–40 indicates habits that can bring about high stress, 20–29 indicates moderate stress, and a score below 20 indicates lo√ stress. Diet and smoking habits are very important to consider in looking at the whole person.

lunch or eating a proper breakfast. Dietary habits have long been known to be an important cause of stress, combined with smoking. The smoke-filled room, plenty of pastries or biscuits and gallons of coffee are potentially damaging to your health. Check your nutritional rating in Box 26.

One way to monitor your stress level is through bio-feedback using a special machine. Or you could carry a small plastic stress indicator card. When you place your finger and thumb on a black square it changes colour – blue for relaxed, green for calm, red for tense and black for stressed. The stress card is fun to use and guaranteed to keep you thinking about stress and to get others talking about the subject. But how far it really measures stress is unclear, so do not treat it too seriously.

A more systematic way of measuring stress is by maintaining a Stress Log in which you note daily any anxiety creating incidents. This provides information about the types of event, person or situation creating difficulties at work and your view of how much stress it caused. A personal Stress Log is shown in Chart 15.

After keeping the log for a few weeks you use the Stress Analysis sheet in Chart 16 to make three separate lists of HIGH, MEDIUM, AND LOW stress events, along with their respective reasons. You thus become more aware of causal factors. Against each event you also indicate 'Possible Counter Measures'. With this information you can begin devising an action plan.

It is not only important to identify and tackle causes of stress at work, it is equally important to maintain a good diet, exercise and activities which give you a sense of calm and inner peace. Outside the office follow whatever seems to work for you to gain a sense of calmness, whether it is fishing or fell walking, reading or some other hobby. Meditation, aerobics, and autogenic training are all highly effective in handling stress.

Distance learning has become increasingly popular; you can buy various programmes teaching you to cope with stress, one of the most successful of which is called Clinically Standardized Meditation (CSM), devised by American psychologist Dr Patricia Carrington. CSM consists of three audio tapes and a tuition book and teaches a simple meditation technique that is free of any religious or spiritual message. It has been tested on thousands of people and been well documented as producing a sense of calm and inner peace which is neither difficult nor lengthy to learn.

Midwest Research (Europe) approaches stress rather differently, offering a one hour audio cassette containing 80–110,000 subliminally recorded repeated phrases on stress control. The inaudible

Chart 15

Personal stress log

SOCIAL SERVICES
DEPARTMENT

DATE _____

7:00 :15 :30 :45	
8:00 :15 :30 :45	
9:00 :15 :30 :45	
10:00 :15 :30 :45	
11:00 :15 :30 :45	
12:00 :15 :30 :45	
1:00 :15 :30 :45	
2:00 :15 :30 :45	
3:00 :15 :30 :45	
4:00 :15 :30 :45	
5:00 :15 :30 :45	

Chart 16

Stress analysis

SOCIAL SERVICES
DEPARTMENT

LEVEL OF STRESS *HIGH/MEDIUM/LOW* _____

	Stress Events	Reasons	Possible Counter Measures
1			
2			
3			
4			
5			
6			
7			
8			
9			
10			
11			
12			
13			
14			
15			
16			
17			
18			
19			
20			

messages apparently bypass the conscious, judgemental mind, going directly to the subconscious level where the most impact is achieved.

According to the company the subliminal messages are worded in such a way as to convince the subconscious that they are true. With sufficient exposure new perceptions emerge to begin producing the intended results. This is the basis of brain washing and since subliminal advertising has long been illegal, the power of such training techniques should not be underestimated. How far it really works with stress remains hard to judge.

With the subliminal tapes all you recognize is the gentle sound of the sea. You play them whenever you want at home or work. They are used daily for several weeks, by which time presumably your main source of stress is the irritating and boring sea sound.

Women managers seem more likely to have higher Type A behaviour patterns than male managers and be even more vulnerable to coronary disease. So that they can manage their Type A behaviour rather than suffer its adverse consequences, cardiologists Friedman and Rosenman suggest a nine-point plan for women, as shown in Box 27.

Impact on others

Relying on only one particular technique to handle change and its associated stress factors is unlikely to be successful. Two main approaches seem possible. The first is to minimize the actual occurrence of stress factors, even though their causes are extremely varied. A survey of the management literature on this subject reveals over 40 interacting factors, many of which require complicated solutions, such as redesigning jobs, altering reward systems, establishing health control programmes, guaranteeing security of tenure and so on.

The second approach is to help people handle their own stress more effectively. Such efforts are increasingly recognized as relevant and worthwhile, although of course there are some managers who do not see the point, and are themselves almost impervious to stress. They are the people who probably cause a considerable amount of stress in their subordinates. Stress to them is something that happens to other people.

Do women need different help to men? Women in organizations, particularly those in managerial roles, often feel that they lack control or power over their work environment and quite a few organizations now offer courses on assertiveness as a way of tackling these problems (see also Chapter 20 on Verbal Skills).

Apart from formal courses on stress management, organizations

Box 27

A nine-point plan for women Type A managers

1 Try and control your obsessional time-directed life:
   By making yourself aware of it and changing the established pattern of behaviour

2 Restrain yourself from trying to be the centre of attention:
   By not constantly talking, particularly when there is no real need to do so

3 Develop reflective periods in your self created hectic programme for life and assess the causes of your 'hurry' sickness

4 Most of your work does not require immediate action. Tell yourself at least once a day that no enterprise ever failed because it was executed too slowly, too well

5 Indulge in outside activities, theatre, reading etc, to lessen obsessional, time orientated behaviour

6 Try not to make unnecessary appointments and impossible deadlines

7 Protect your time, learn to say no

8 Take as many stress free breathing spaces during the course of an intensive working day as possible

9 Try to create opportunities during the day or night when you can entirely relax your body and mind

---

often develop their own programmes. There has also been a growing realization that team building can be a major contributor to reducing stress through sharing anxieties and peer group support.

You need therefore to be alert to stress symptoms in your subordinates. For example, someone who argues with you more than usual, or a person who is normally assertive and who becomes unusually quiet, may be suffering from stress. As their manager it is your job to take an interest. Similarly, people who start smoking, or take an increasing amount of sick leave, or whose work suddenly deteriorates, may all be suffering from stress. Making time for regular supervisory sessions is one way of learning whether a person is suffering unduly from stress. Your subordinate may not directly admit it, but talk instead of 'having too much work' or 'not enough time to do all the things I have to do' or 'there's so much happening at the moment' and so on.

If you suspect that subordinates are suffering from stress resulting from the impact of change there are various important contributions you can make which are summarized in Box 28.

When actively engaged in bringing about change you may easily forget that your own actions are a source of stress for other people. For example, if as head of a department you are busily engaged in restructuring, altering people's roles, work relationships and jobs, you may lose sight of the fact that those on the receiving end may be experiencing a profound sense of loss. Your plans may be introducing role ambiguity through lack of information about how people will perform their new roles. In particular, role ambiguity is created when:

- Work objectives are unclear

- There is uncertainty about what others expect of us now and tomorrow

- The scope and responsibility of jobs are unclear.

Even when uncertainty is resolved, people may still require what amounts to a period of 'mourning' as they come to terms with losing their old associations and ways of working and adapt to new ones. When you are enthusiastic about the changes you are introducing, it can be frustrating when some people keep referring to past ways of doing things, or seem to want to keep meeting during working hours with colleagues who are no longer directly concerned with their new work patterns.

These behaviours though are all part of the process of adaptation. Patience and understanding will gradually help people come to terms with the new situation. Attempting to suppress these sorts of behaviour, for example by banning certain meetings, or denying the value of previous ways of working, may merely arouse resentment and resistance and delay the time when the change really takes hold.

To handle change well you need to take account of this need to 'mourn' and allow space for people to share feelings and provide mutual support to each other.

Box 28

Strategies for minimizing stress during a time of change

STAFF DEVELOPMENT

- HELP people reduce the stress they often place on themselves by adopting realistic goals
- ENCOURAGE people to adopt new goals that give alternative sources of satisfaction
- PROVIDE opportunities for in-service training designed to increase role effectiveness and adapt to change
- ENSURE that stress levels are monitored either in management supervision sessions or some other way
- OFFER work-focussed counselling or consultation for those who are experiencing stress
- ENCOURAGE the development of mutual support groups or networks

JOBS AND ROLES

- ASSIST others to review their work load and priorities; where relevant consider how to reduce work loads, temporarily or permanently
- SPREAD difficult or unrewarding work equitably
- INCREASE opportunities at every level to exercise judgement, enhancing people's feelings of competence, ability to cope, to use skills to make decisions
- STRUCTURE roles and team arrangements to allow 'time out' sessions to occur
- CONSIDER using extra personnel to ease pressures during the transition phase of change
- INSIST that people take their holidays
- DISCOURAGE frequent weekend and regular late night working
- CHECK to what extent people with subordinates are delegating
- CLARIFY roles and responsibilities during a period of major change
- BUILD career ladders

MANAGEMENT DEVELOPMENT

- DEVELOP training which focusses on current major problems
- MONITOR performance and give regular feedback
- WATCH for stress, intervene when strain is excessive

ORGANIZATIONAL MECHANISMS

- DO NOT change everything at once; leave a stable and secure base from which new arrangements can be explored
- GIVE adequate time and resources to project teams and their leaders charged with implementing change
- CREATE formal ways to encourage group and organizational problem solving
- PROMOTE involvement by maximizing people's autonomy and participation in the change process
- FORMALIZE ways of handling conflict
- ENSURE adequate and direct feedback about new methods
- DEVELOP clear organizational goals and distinct values

GUIDELINES

- BALANCE commitment to the change objectives and your own health and your family's

- DECIDE whether you tend towards Type A or Type B behaviour

- ASCERTAIN your own stress level regularly

- DO not neglect simple health requirements like exercise, taking a break for lunch or eating a proper breakfast; review diet and reduce, preferably eliminate, smoking

- TRY the nine-point plan for reducing stress if you are a woman manager

- USE team building to improve stress handling

- WATCH for stress symptoms in subordinates

- REMEMBER that YOU may be a cause of stress!

- ALLOW time and space for 'mourning' the loss of what existed before the change

- MINIMIZE stress by methods such as those shown in Box 28.

Procedures
13. Outside agents

'What's the time?'

'Lend me your watch and I'll tell you!'

This quip can be related to the way many people see the work of outside consultants – they get paid to tell you what you already know. A more cynical opinion is that they only report convenient truths, rather than uncomfortable facts. How else can they operate if they are to stay in business? Messengers bringing unpleasant news are seldom invited back. In direct contrast to the idea that consultants are useless is the belief that major organizational change is dependent on a master blueprint, best created with the help of an omniscient consultant or change agent.

It is certainly right to be sceptical of what outside change agents can offer. Why use one when the same results can often be achieved by people already in the company? Senior managers commonly under-rate the skills that exist in-house.

However, outsiders can be especially useful in identifying and tackling situations which are spiralling downward:

Chart 17

Low performance and expectations

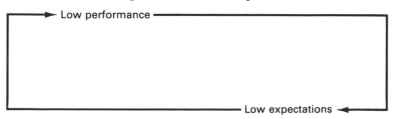

Having identified this situation an outside agent attempts to turn it into one based on high expectations and high performance. Some of the problems of using outsiders and the advantages of using insiders are shown in Box 29. There may be particular benefits in having outsiders work with a selected group of internal change agents. In the Metal Box company, for example, attaching some internal staff to work with consultants produced these benefits:

- Reduced fee or shorter time scale

- Less disruption to operations, because seconded staff were able to spot potential problems early

- A resource of people able to understand the consultant's work and thus able to trouble-shoot after the consultant has left

- A pool of people able to apply similar techniques to other issues.

Box 29

Using inside or outside change agents

Disadvantages of an outside change agent	Advantages of an inside change agent
Is a stranger	Knows the system, where power lies, and opinion leaders, and the strategic leverage points
May not identify with the problems	
Takes time to fully understand values, culture and way organization works	Speaks the organization's language – the special way members refer to things, tone, and style of discussing things
May create dependency	
Can generate resistance	Understands the norms and commonly held beliefs, attitudes and behaviours
Cost	
Adverse impact on morale, indicating lack of management confidence in existing staff	

Types of change agent

Anyone who alters the *status quo* within an organization is a change agent. A consultant who is hired to do a particular piece of work on a fixed contract and then leaves once the work is completed, is the simplest type of change agent. On the other hand some consultants have permanent contracts, becoming virtually part of the organization's staff, perhaps on a part-time basis.

British Airways, for instance, brought in a number of outside consultants to supplement internal consulting staff for several years to assist in a massive staff development programme. Equally, an outside change agent could be someone from one part of the organization intervening in a different part to alter the *status quo*.

Outside change agents broadly fall into two categories, those concerned with process and those offering a techniques package. Those concerned with process study what is happening, with no set solution in mind. An example would be an organizational development specialist diagnosing a situation to enable managers to implement their own solutions.

Those offering a 'package' of know-how deliver a known result, as, for example, consultants who design and install appraisal systems, employee incentive schemes, computerized personnel records and so on. More specifically there are people change agents, analysis change agents and organization development agents as shown in Box 30.

Box 30

Outside change agents

People change agents produce programmes directly affecting how people in the organization behave; focus on worker motivation and morale, using a variety of techniques such as management by objectives, job enrichment, reward systems and so on.

Analysis change agents concentrate on altering the technology and organizational structure to improve efficiency and output, the use of new technology or production techniques; may also be active in forming new task groups within the organization to install and operate innovations.

Organization development agents examine who relates to whom, how people work together, the values and culture of the organization, and issues such as leadership and decision making; may have a particular commitment to working in depth on team and interpersonal effectiveness.

Change agents alter the *status quo* and create new situations in which people must relearn their roles. This factor alone explains why they are sometimes feared and resisted. Outsiders usually have less to lose in proposing major shifts which is often why they are used, and there may be justification for permanent employees fearing that their arrival heralds major cut backs, job losses and adverse career moves.

Getting the best from an outside agent

Using an external change agent will not guarantee either comfortable or even successful results. It is therefore important to maximize the chances that a planned outside intervention will succeed. The following checklist questions can help here:

What values does the change agent hold and will these be discussed?

A strength and weakness of outside agents is that they bring their own values to the task. It is important to clarify these values in the early stages since they may have a fundamental impact on how the agent tackles the problem and on the agent's acceptability. For example, a catering consultant committed to the concept of privatizing council services would not gain much credibility if hired by a council politically opposed to the idea.

How will conflicts between the change agent's values and those of the client be handled?

You cannot expect an outside agent to have identical views to your own or those of the organization – there are bound to be differences. An outsider who is committed to achieving change primarily through involving employees may discover that the management does not value participation and is unwilling to alter its approach. How such differences are handled are as important as the existence of the differences themselves. Discover how the consultant would proceed when such differences arise. It is unhelpful, for instance, if the consultant's approach would be to press on regardless or, if faced with opposition, to resign.

What strategies will the change agent consider using?

Before signing the contract, it is important to ask the consultant how he would tackle your particular situation so that you can obtain an idea of how he develops a strategy for tackling problems. Are there any strategies the change agent would be reluctant or refuse to use?

A consultant will usually bring to the task a 'kit bag' of change techniques. While there is nothing wrong with such an armoury of techniques, you may find yourself paying simply because of them. It is important that they are not applied blindly to the problem or forced to fit the situation simply because the consultant is happy using a particular tried and tested approach. For instance, a consultant with a commitment to, or experience of, appraisal systems may find it hard to avoid recommending the installation of such a system. Similarly, asked to consult on computerizing some aspect of the organization, outside computer consultants tend to favour a particular software programme or piece of hardware.

How long is the change agent prepared to continue the relationship?
Consultants are usually sensitive to any suggestion that they might merely submit reports leaving you with the problem of implementation. A simple reassurance is not enough. Spend time clarifying the time horizon of the outside change agent and determine how far you are expecting the change agent to lead the implementation, which is primarily a management task.

Will the change agent present options for change?
There is usually more than one way of achieving a particular result and the routes by which the end state is reached should be stated in terms of management choices. For example, there may be cost and human implications in the size and pace of a particular change. There may also be significant choices about implementation. An outside change agent examining how to introduce a computerized personnel information system, for instance, should indicate the implications of choosing between a system that is independent of the existing payroll suite and one which is based on it.

Will the change agent indicate the reasons for change and the supporting evidence?
Recommended changes should be based on evidence which can be evaluated and the reasoning behind arriving at a particular approach should be explained.

What is the link between the change actions and the end result?
The organization is probably paying hundreds of pounds per day for an outside agent's efforts and is entitled to see a justification for the proposals. For instance, a consultant who suggests a major programme of team building should demonstrate first that there is a problem which demands team building, and secondly how team building will actually deliver the results which managers want.

Will the change agent clarify goals and objectives to all concerned?
Too often consultants talk of 'increased efficiency' or tell you that 'you will really only see the benefits in the long run', without quantifying what these notional gains will be. In the early stages of using an outside change agent, particularly ones concerned with techniques rather than process, work needs to be done to clarify roles, working procedures and expected outcomes.
　　Ascertain also what responsibility the outside change agent will

assume for communicating goals and objectives to those who need to know. Management may leave this task to the consultant while the latter expects managers to do it.

What freedom will the consultant have to decide goals of change; means of implementation; and how change will be tracked?
Consultants or outside change agents are often presented with a broad statement of the problem and simply asked to return with answers. This can be costly and time consuming if the brief is not really as open as it is made tó appear.

Leaving the implementation of change to the outsider or others lower down in the organization may appear to be democratic. In practice, it removes those in power from direct involvement in a process that calls for strong guidance and actual support. Ensure that those calling in the consultants stay closely in touch with the change effort.

Ask for references and follow these up
Enquire about the change agent's record of cost against estimate; about the relationship with internal people; whether there is a tendency to introduce inexperienced learners once the contract is landed; and whether other clients would use the outsider again.

Of particular concern is how the change agent handles matters of confidentiality. Does the change agent, for example, understand the limits of the brief? One firm which hired a consultant from a well known institute found that the consultant also brought in two less experienced colleagues. The latter decided to write a supplementary and unrequested report on problems which they had identified in how the organization operated. This report was presented without the agreement of the organization's project manager and caused considerable dismay over its contents. The two inexperienced change agents had behaved unethically and when confronted did not really understand the limits of their remit.

Change agent principles

How consultants or outside change agents create change may be little different to the way in which managers themselves proceed, except for particular skills or know-how. The style used, though, may be different and in deciding whether or not to use a particular change agent check that they will adapt to your own organizational style and approach. You can do this by asking for a demonstration of skills or experience in the areas shown in Box 31.

Box 31

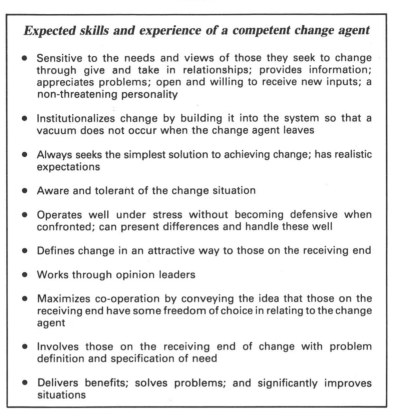

Expected skills and experience of a competent change agent

- Sensitive to the needs and views of those they seek to change through give and take in relationships; provides information; appreciates problems; open and willing to receive new inputs; a non-threatening personality

- Institutionalizes change by building it into the system so that a vacuum does not occur when the change agent leaves

- Always seeks the simplest solution to achieving change; has realistic expectations

- Aware and tolerant of the change situation

- Operates well under stress without becoming defensive when confronted; can present differences and handle these well

- Defines change in an attractive way to those on the receiving end

- Works through opinion leaders

- Maximizes co-operation by conveying the idea that those on the receiving end have some freedom of choice in relating to the change agent

- Involves those on the receiving end of change with problem definition and specification of need

- Delivers benefits; solves problems; and significantly improves situations

Outside change agents, and consultants in particular, are neither as parasitical nor as powerful as the myths about them suggest. But they can play a key role in the management of planned, that is deliberate, change. At some time in your management career you may have contact with outside agents, so it is worth knowing how to obtain the best from them.

GUIDELINES

- CLARIFY the values held by the change agent

- AGREE on how conflicts between the values of the change agent and those of the client will be handled

- DETERMINE how the outside agent would go about tackling the particular situation

- DISCOVER whether there are any strategies the change agent would be reluctant or refuse to use

- STATE the time horizon for the work of the outside change agent

- RESOLVE how far you are expecting the change agent to lead the implementation of change

- ENSURE that the way in which the end result is to be achieved is subject to management choices

- SEEK enough information to understand why recommended changes are made and the link between them and the end result

- CLARIFY with the outside agent roles, working procedures and expected outcomes

- DEFINE the responsibility for communicating goals and objectives to those who need to know

- DETERMINE what freedom the outside agent will have to decide change goals; means of implementation; and how change will be tracked

- ASK for references and follow these up

- CHECK that the outside agent has the required skills and experience as shown in Box 31.

Procedures
14. Tracking

Driving a racing car is good for you. Philips, the world's second largest electronics firm, wanted their executives to absorb the lessons from life in the fast lane. So they sent selected managers to a motor racing school to underline what lay behind the company's change programme: the will to win, competitive instincts and getting it right first time.

The racing car experience was the logical extension of the firm's tracking of past changes. After years of messing with its structure, during the early 1980s Philips reviewed its strengths and weaknesses. Nobody liked what they saw. Profits were sluggish, some market shares were vulnerable to competition and inefficiencies were rife. Decision making was slow, production systems were costly and no one really understood the links between research, product development, and marketing. Philips was not using its strengths to become highly competitive.

Evaluating the previous changes led to a new company mission: 'to increase our profitability in order to maintain leadership in key sectors of the electronics industry'. A strategy for achieving this was devised consisting of clear organizational goals:

- Philips must be a global company with products and production for a global market

- Strategy must be directed by a central policy and planning process

- Top priority must be given to the development and strengthening of the core activities

- Utilization of resources must be improved.

For Philips to become a global concern, its managers would have to emulate racing drivers by moving fast, beating their rivals and doing things superbly well. By late 1987 the President and Chairman was pointing to a healthier organization. He could answer the basic question applicable to every change effort: have we done what we said we'd do?

In its simplicity the Philips' mission statement and its accompanying strategy was strikingly similar to that selected by the management team at the Woolworth retail chain of shops: 'To be the most profitable retail stores group in the country'. Though still some way from achieving its declared mission the Woolworth team were able to demonstrate enough substantial progress to shareholders to help resist an unwelcome takeover bid from Dixons.

Monitoring and evaluation

When we track the change effort we are monitoring and evaluating. Monitoring is a continuous process of discovering what is happening, what is going off track, what people think, what needs doing next and so on. It is relatively low key and usually relies on limited information.

By contrast, evaluation is infrequent and more judgemental. It generally requires extensive information from, for example, existing and new record systems, structured and unstructured interviews, observations and so on. Specialists may be needed to organize the evaluation, make judgements about outcomes, assess how well something was done and how to do better next time. Because of the information demands, the need for rigorous analysis and the complexity of the task, evaluations can be expensive and time consuming and may raise more questions than they answer.

Whether you are attempting monitoring or evaluating, tracking change seeks to answer:

● WHAT IS HAPPENING?

● DID WE DO WHAT WE SAID WE'D DO?

● WHAT CAN WE LEARN FROM HOW WE DID IT?

● WHERE DO WE GO FROM HERE?

What is happening?

Napoleon claimed that no plan survives the battle. With organizational change reality also ensures unexpected, perhaps unwanted, outcomes. Some of these may be minimized, even avoided if corrective action is taken at the right time. So tracking deals with outcomes and also with discovering what is happening during the entire change process. The change process is shown in Chart 18.

Tracking allows managers to review how the change is going, right from its inception through to the adjustments that inevitably occur once change is underway.

If tracking is to be useful you need to know in advance 'what ought to be happening?' Thus, for instance, had the Philips' management team found that the utilization of resources was actually worsening, it would have suggested new corrective action. Knowing what ought to happen stems from being clear about the desired end state.

Chart 18

The change process

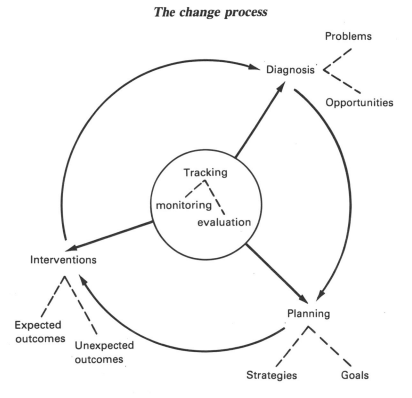

Did we do what we said we'd do?

Most change efforts begin with no clear sense of direction, progress to weak plans and are characterized by excessive optimism about the results. More than half of all new technology projects, for example, fail to deliver the benefits expected; the bulk of company takeovers produce fewer gains than originally envisaged; and most restructuring seems to damage somebody.

Evaluation of outcomes can be worthless, however, if managers are too far into the next change effort, or if it would be too difficult to unravel the past. Evaluation may even be damaging to the actual change process. If you keep pulling up a plant to check if its roots are growing you can hardly expect it to survive!

Evaluating outcomes to learn whether 'we did what we said we'd do' is worth attempting if:

- The original change objectives were reasonably clear

- Enough people want to know the results

- It is feasible and economic

- It will help dispel the myth that the change effort has failed

- The results might suggest what to do next.

Objectives

It is one of the myths of managing major change that the objectives have to be tightly specified and preferably quantitative. This is not confirmed by successful change orientated organizations, particularly those which are good at innovating. Change objectives merely need to be clear, understandable and capable of being related to outcomes so that managers can answer the question: 'have we succeeded or failed?'

People want to know

Enough people in the organization must want the evaluation results to justify its time and expense. Often managers would rather not probe too deeply into the change effort in case the answers they uncover are unwelcome. Usually what will sway people to back an evaluation programme is whether the results of evaluation will be available soon enough to guide future action. In Philips, for instance, evaluating past changes was recognized as essential if new directions were to be identified and made acceptable across the organization.

Feasible

The viability, timing and cost of an evaluation effort must all be right. First, an evaluation must be possible to undertake. Given the complexity of many change efforts evaluation may not prove practical. Secondly, an evaluation must begin at the right time. If it is started too early in the change process, there will be no way of deciding whether 'we have done what we said we would do': on the other hand, waiting until the change effort has almost been forgotten undermines evaluation. The best timing is when the answers will arrive in time to influence future decisions. Thirdly, the costs must be acceptable for the return expected from the evaluation.

Myths

When a change effort is undertaken there will always be those who remain convinced that the old ways were better and who prefer the previous *status quo*. It may also take a considerable time before all the benefits from the change begin to show. Consequently, individuals or groups may persist in looking backwards to the period before the change. The idea may prevail that somehow the change has not been a success. In these circumstances, evaluation can be some help in demonstrating the reality and identifying where the change has produced worthwhile results.

Results suggest what to do next

Worthwhile evaluation must point to future action, being a baseline from which to decide new courses of action. For example, if a firm discovers that, having sought to capture 50 per cent of a market, it has only acquired a third; then an analysis of the reason for its partial success may offer guidance for corrective action. Evaluation helps us to:

Avoid making that mistake again!

Learn how to repeat our successes!

Knowing what went wrong with a particular change effort, and why, may prevent us making the same mistake twice. For example, one company conducted an evaluation into its recent restructuring and learned that late into the change effort an extensive team building effort had been required to handle problems created by the new structure. Team building should have occurred much earlier, but having learned this the company never repeated this mistake.

When a change effort has been highly successful evaluation can be an investment in learning how to repeat it. For instance, an analysis of the restructuring of roles within one company showed that people liked the new arrangements and felt that the transition stage had been about the right length, removing damaging uncertainty. This provided a useful indicator for future changes in respect of timing and the transition stage.

Openly asking 'what can we learn from how we did it?' conveys that management is listening to what people think, inspiring confidence in the next round of changes.

Where do we go from here?

Evaluation helps decide what to do next by revealing whether the change effort is on course. Since organizational goals are continually changing, it may be relevant at any time during the change process. It is more important to establish what to do next than to conduct a perfect evaluation. Driving many organizational changes is a management vision of the future. Evaluation shows whether the organization is still moving towards this vision or whether the pace is slowing.

A plan

Having decided to evaluate a change effort how do you go about it? Since change efforts vary so widely it is only possible to identify the broad outline of what should happen, as shown in Box 32.

Box 32

Creating an evaluation plan
STEP 1   DEFINE 'the customer' – Who 'owns' responsibility for acting on the eventual results?
STEP 2   CLARIFY purpose or priorities for evaluation, ensure 'customer' agreement
STEP 3   DECIDE when to evaluate; methods of data collection and analysis
STEP 4   SPECIFY and commit resources needed and available, and role of staff
STEP 5   DETERMINE information required and sources
STEP 6   LIST who will receive data from evaluation

Tracking, particularly evaluation, produces large amounts of data which managers must analyse and interpret. It is extremely useful to have a road map which guides the process. One such road map is called Stream Analysis.

Stream Analysis

Stream Analysis is the invention of Dr Jerry Porras, consultant and associate professor at Stanford University. Using charts to show what is happening at any time during the change effort, Stream Analysis assumes that organizations consist of different, interconnected sub systems.

As Chapter 1 on Models indicates, it can be difficult to make sense of all the relationships which are produced by seeing the organization as an open system. Even so Stream Analysis tries to chart the interconnections. It can be used by a single manager or preferably a small team responsible for guiding the change effort. Four components lie at the heart of Stream Analysis and are the setting in which change occurs:

- Organizational arrangements

- Social factors

- Technology

- Physical setting.

Organizational problems are collected and allocated to one of these four settings. Attempts are made to trace the links by examining whether one problem seems to be causing another; whether one problem is related to another with no evidence of a causal link; whether a problem both causes and is caused by another; and whether there is a clear and reasonably significant relationship between one problem and another.

Stream Analysis was applied by a manager in a large community hospital that had been expanding fast for six years and was experiencing problems with its Nursing Assistants (NAs). Absenteeism existed, turnover was high, and job performance was poor. Persistent issues needing a concerted attack are highlighted in Chart 19.

Lack of adequate technical standards and procedures emerged as a core issue along with three other slightly less critical ones. Instead of making scapegoats of the Nursing Assistants the causes

Chart 19

Stream analysis

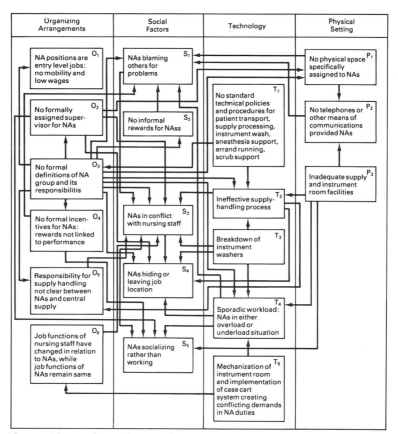

Source: J Porras, *Stream Analysis,* © 1987, Addison-Wesley Publishing Co., Inc., Reading, Massachusetts. Reprinted with permission.

of the human problems were identified. An action plan was devised and implemented, the changes being tracked using the Stream Analysis technique.

The steps for conducting Stream Analysis are shown in Box 33. They offer managers a practical way of tracking change and uncovering what has been done, so that the organization can learn how to change itself more effectively.

Box 33

Stream analysis steps
1 Form a change management team
2 Collect information on issues in the organization
3 Categorize and place issues on a Stream Chart
4 On the chart draw interconnections among issues
5 Analyse and identify core problems, stories and themes
6 Create a Stream Planning Chart to guide actions prescribed by the diagnosis
7 Implement the plan
8 Document intervention activity on a Stream Tracking Chart

GUIDELINES

- DISTINGUISH between monitoring or evaluating the change effort

- SET clear change objectives to assist in tracking

- USE the four tracking questions:
  What is happening?
  Did we do what we said we'd do?
  What can we learn from how we did it?
  Where do we go from here?

- CONSIDER tracking only if:
  The answer might suggest what to do next
  Change objectives were reasonably clearly specified
  Enough people want the results
  It is feasible and economic
  It will help dispel the myth that the change effort has failed

- DEVELOP a systematic evaluation plan

- TRY using Stream Analysis to unravel the complexities of the change effort.

Techniques
15. Force Field Analysis

Force Field Analysis (FFA) helps analyse situations that you want to change. Using it you can tackle seemingly immovable obstacles to change. The technique has been around for decades, outlasting many other management aids. As a tool of great resilience, it continues to be taught on management courses.

Generations of working managers have found FFA simple to understand, easy to use and that it works. It starts by assuming that:

At any given moment, any situation in an organization is in a state of equilibrium.

This is a version of the physical sciences' law that a body will be at rest when all the forces acting on it cancel each other out. This does not mean that everything is locked into a static state or permanent *status quo*. In an organization there is dynamic tension between a whole set of counteracting forces that maintain the *status quo* (see Chart 20 below).

Some of the forces push towards goal achievement, others oppose it. Suppose some specialist staff in an organization decide that they should be paid more. They have many forces pushing them to obtain this goal, such as extra work being thrust on them, longer working hours, market demand for their skills, family pressures, inflation and so on. There may be equally strong counter forces, such as the wish of management to restrain further wage rises, the wish of other staff to preserve differentials, the desire not to let this group of specialists become too important, and so on.

Change is possible only when one or both of the following occur:

Restraining forces weaken

Driving forces strengthen.

There are consequently two distinct if sometimes complementary routes to making things happen. It may be feasible to strengthen

Chart 20

Analysing the forces

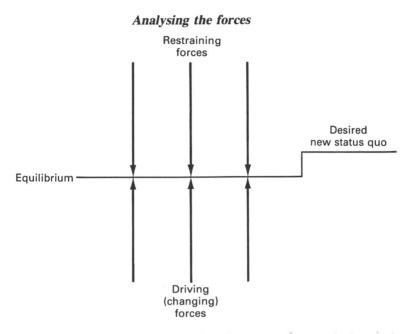

the driving forces pushing the situation towards a particular goal. For instance, the specialists in the above example might make themselves even more indispensible by taking on important new roles or projects.

If it is impossible to increase the driving forces then perhaps it may be feasible to weaken the restraining forces which are preventing change. In the above example the specialists might let it be known that they are all job hunting, which may weaken management's resolve to resist change. Or the managers might strengthen the resisting forces by limiting dependence on the specialists by subcontracting some work to outside suppliers.

When the equilibrium of driving and restraining forces is disturbed, that is the forces become out of balance, change occurs towards, or away from, the desired goal. Once this happens the situation may continue moving in unexpected ways by:

A return to the previous *status quo*

Reaching some entirely different goal.

The management of change first requires an unfreezing of the balanced set of forces maintaining the *status quo*, then with the establishment of a new and desired equilibrium making it permanent or refreezing. Otherwise powerful forces may undermine the change, causing a return to the old *status quo*. The process is shown in simplified form in Chart 21 below:

Chart 21

Making change stick

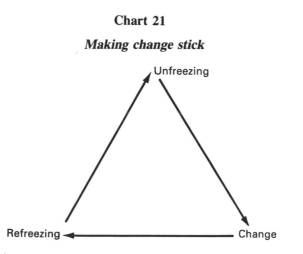

For example, when a manager or outside change agent who has introduced important organization changes departs, there may be powerful forces which gradually reverse the changes unless they have been 'frozen' into place.

This view of the change as a process of unfreezing, and then refreezing, is less acceptable today since we are more conscious of the dynamics of the change process. New equilibriums are rare in a period of great change. Situations are constantly altering and the aim of refreezing, although attractive, is unrealistic. Force Field Analysis does, however, provide a useful way of focussing attention on the power of driving and restraining forces.

Diagnosis

Using FFA is a combination of defining the problem or situation carefully followed by reviewing the driving and restraining forces to see how to affect them. The power of FFA lies in affecting at least one of the forces. The main steps in using FFA are summarized below.

Step 1   State the problem area

Define the broad topic area, such as issues concerned with

personnel, marketing, production, administration and so on. The problem must be a real one, important to you and worth trying to resolve. The problem area defines the boundaries of the situation which you want to alter.

Step 2   Define the situation

Next state the situation to be changed in order to describe the *status quo*. For example, a group of foremen may make a PROBLEM AREA STATEMENT that they are concerned about output quality. To DEFINE THE SITUATION they go further and state specifically that the present reject rate of 20 per cent is unacceptable.

Because a problem defined is often a problem half solved, it pays to spend time producing a tight specification of the situation. How big is the problem, how important is it, where is it located, who or what is involved with it, was there a time when the problem did not exist?

Step 3   Specify the goal

Now you define the new situation which you want to reach. This is a goal, a statement of how the situation would look if the blocks to change were removed and a new *status quo* was achieved.

It can be helpful to express the goal in quantified form or at least provide some measurable way of deciding whether the goal has actually been achieved. In the above example the foremen decide that their goal is to achieve zero defects. Defining both the *status quo* and the goal produces a picture of the gap due to the current equilibrium of driving and restraining forces.

Step 4   Analyse the forces

Now create two separate lists showing restraining and driving forces. These lists may come from a mixture of brainstorming and more detailed research. You are only interested in forces already at work, not ones which might arise in the future or have ceased to exist. You can also classify each force into: STRONG; MEDIUM; or WEAK. The information will fall into four main types as shown in Chart 22.

This analysis should allow you to decide where to begin affecting the *status quo* by influencing the various forces. You may, for instance, conclude that it is better to affect those falling in area A rather than waste time on those in Area B. Similarly you may conclude that restraining forces in the C area are too difficult to

Chart 22
Analysing the forces

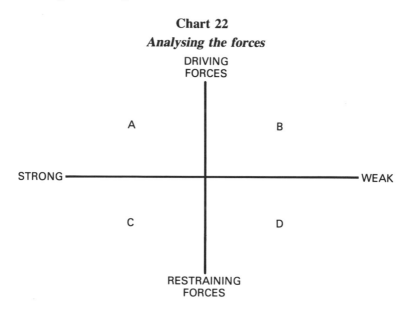

influence and that it is more sensible to spend time weakening forces in the D area.

In defining the forces you need to be specific. A statement such as 'opposition from senior management' may need refining into: 'The Assistant Chief Executive opposes the project'. Or, 'lack of regular feedback' may need hardening to: 'We never receive praise when we do things well'.

When describing a complicated force it may need breaking down into its components to make it easier to decide what might be done. For example, a restraining force such as 'poor marketing support' may need subdividing into: 'irregular market surveys'; 'marketing department not in regular contact'; 'marketing director gives weak support to experimenting with new promotional ideas'.

To examine the various forces in further depth you can also categorize them into:

- PERSONAL FORCES – anything which refers to you, such as attitudes, feelings, weaknesses, relationships, education, income and so on

- RELATIONSHIP FORCES – how different individuals and groups relate to each other, such as the organization and government, the department and other departments, the team and other teams and so on

- SYSTEM FORCES – factors that form the organization's environment including political, social, legal, environmental, local conditions and so on.

It is helpful to draw a visual impression of the various forces pushing for and against change. For example, Chart 23 shows an analysis of a situation in the welfare field. The PROBLEM AREA is inter-agency planning and provision of services for carers (that is people who look after elderly or handicapped relatives at home).

Chart 23

Force Field Analysis in action

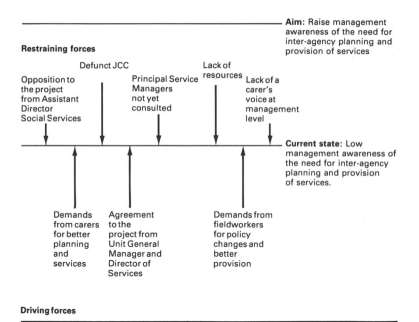

Aim: Raise management awareness of the need for inter-agency planning and provision of services

Restraining forces

Defunct JCC

Lack of resources

Opposition to the project from Assistant Director Social Services

Principal Service Managers not yet consulted

Lack of a carer's voice at management level

Current state: Low management awareness of the need for inter-agency planning and provision of services.

Demands from carers for better planning and services

Agreement to the project from Unit General Manager and Director of Services

Demands from fieldworkers for policy changes and better provision

Driving forces

Source: Action for Carers, Kings Fund, 1988

The DEFINITION OF THE SITUATION is the low management awareness of the need for inter-agency planning and provision of services; the GOAL is to raise awareness about it. The various restraining and driving forces are shown at the head of each arrow. A further sophistication would be to vary the lengths of the arrows to reflect the strength or weakness of the forces which they represent.

Step 5   Devise a strategy

Think carefully about your strategy for altering the *status quo*. For instance, by increasing driving forces that threaten or pressure people you may increase resistance to altering the *status quo*. You rarely have enough time or knowledge to influence all the forces, nor is this necessary. With the situation in equilibrium and driving forces exactly matching restraining forces all you need to locate is one force susceptible to your influence. This is like an army commander probing for the enemy's weak spot. It is seldom necessary to find more than one. Thus you choose the force which is easiest to change and has the best result.

It is generally better to strengthen those driving forces that do not increase resistance; or to work to weaken restraining forces; or to consider how new driving forces can be brought into play. Also consider tackling forces which cause the least disruption when altered.

The best strategy may prove to be a mixture of weakening restraining and strengthening driving forces, particularly if you are not sure about the relative importance of the various forces.

Step 6   Develop an action plan

Once you have decided on a strategy for affecting one or more of the forces you need a detailed plan of action. This may consist of many highly practical tasks and these must be treated like any other management aim, in which there is clarity about who will do what, when, and the resources needed to make each task possible. There should also be some criteria by which you can decide if the task has been completed or not.

Keep the various steps in your action plan simple. Go for many small successes rather than one large one. To influence one of the driving or restraining forces your action plan must be followed through with determination and you should always be able to tell whether your individual small steps are succeeding or failing.

Step 7   Establish a new equilibrium

Once you have influenced the driving or restraining forces change is set in motion. Now there is the possibility that events may take an unexpected turn, the original goal being reached and left behind, or an entirely new and perhaps undesirable situation being created. An example of this latter situation is a company which makes a much publicized takeover bid for another firm and, having succeeded, finds itself on the receiving end of unwelcome offers.

Once a new situation has been achieved there is a risk of returning to the previous *status quo*, unless the changes are made irreversible. The implication of using FFA is that efforts must be made to consolidate the change, to refreeze the situation and to create a new, acceptable *status quo*. This may be harder than the original task of disturbing the equilibrium. To institutionalize change the new situation must become part of the fabric of the organization itself.

An example of refreezing a situation is when a manager finds ways to make people 'own' the changes and have a vested interest in maintaining the new situation. If, for instance, a manager introduces a new statistical reporting system for monitoring progress and insists that every month the output from the system is reviewed, this builds it into people's regular thinking habits and work roles.

Why use FFA?

Force Field Analysis provides a simple framework to help people decide what steps they ought to take. Another of its benefits is that it reduces a problem to a 'do-able' size. It also stimulates new ways of taking action. If certain situations seem set in concrete with little likelihood for change, FFA can encourage a more optimistic view, directing a search for those vulnerable points where the right action will tip the balance, starting a move away from the present *status quo*.

A further attraction of FFA is that it can be used by an individual manager or by a large group. The latter will often prove more creative than a single person working alone. It assists a group to get on the same wave length, reach a common understanding of a situation, develop a sense of teamwork and make a commitment to the change goal.

Effective though FFA can be it depends for its success on the quality and completeness of the analysis. For example, if you fail to identify all the main driving and restraining forces you may be faced with selecting one to alter which is particularly difficult when in fact there are easier, unlisted ones, available.

Finally, the clear framework for developing an action plan which is the strength of Force Field Analysis is also its weakness. On occasions it can seem over-analytical and elaborate. Despite this it is a proven aid which can considerably improve the quality of thinking and planning that goes into the change effort.

GUIDELINES

- CREATE separate lists of restraining and driving force

- BREAK down complicated situations into their components with their own driving and restraining forces

- ANALYSE FORCES into whether they deal with personal factors, relationships or systems

- DRAW a visual representation of the various forces involved in maintaining a situation

- FOCUS effort and resources on affecting one force, the 'weak spot' in the situation

- KEEP action plans simple

- SEEK to refreeze, to institutionalize the new situation.

Techniques
16. Sensing

'You need to get under the skin of this organization'; 'One never really knows what people think in this place'; 'I don't have enough contact yet with people in this organization'; 'Recognizing the need to change must go beyond just me'; 'I need some hard data on which to base changes'; 'I must find a way to get my influential senior colleagues convinced of the need for change'; 'I want to tap people's ideas.'

These are just some of the ways in which organizational leaders express the challenge of organizational change. In the cycle of strategic change (see Chart 2, Chapter 1 on Models) the first issue is:

What changes do we need to make – diagnosis?

The greater your power and responsibility the less daily contact you will usually have with people doing much of the work, the ones who make your ideas succeed. How can you discover what changes they see to be relevant?

Ways to diagnose what changes are needed include employee attitude surveys, polling, feedback through the management hierarchy on specific issues, suggestion schemes, market research, and so on. Management by walking around can also be revealing.

There are occasions though when you want to tap systematically into a wide range of views about possible organizational change without using the clinical approach of formal surveys or leaving it to individualistic approaches such as management by walking around. Sensing is a way of learning from people in the organization with whom there is little personal contact. As a diagnostic tool it highlights issues rather than how to deal with them. The two main ways of sensing are:

- VERTICAL SENSING – usually conducted in small groups from an entire vertical slice of the organization

167

- HORIZONTAL SENSING – using participants from no more than three or four levels across the entire organization.

The aim is to identify problems of concern to the chosen groups, whether they be supervisors, middle managers, front line staff, accountants, engineers and so on.

Sensing in action

John Mortimer is general manager of a company employing around 1,500 people. He has produced a clear statement explaining his vision of what sort of organization he wants it to become. His business plan focusses on expanding exports and he particularly wants to uncover ways of improving the company's general performance. He needs the commitment of his senior managers and the rest of their staff if the vision and business plan are to become a reality. He is acutely aware that an upward flow of unfiltered information is hard to achieve. It is easier to send information downward than to draw it from below.

Achieving any organizational change requires energy and commitment. This is especially so when you are wanting to turn a general awareness of problems and opportunities into positive action. Transforming a feeling that change is needed into a widely held view demands credible data. The act of collecting such data can itself influence people to accept that a major change is justified.

John Mortimer has heard about Sensing and decides that it is appropriate for him to use. He asks his deputy to schedule 10 meetings, each 90 minutes long, with different groups of employees. To gain a 'feel' for what people throughout the organization think, the two managers decide to invite a mix of staff:

Group 1:   Non-supervisory, technical and office employees

Group 2:   Professional employees and staff specialists

Group 3:   Supervisors

Group 4:   Cross-sections of employees – one person from each organizational level, and no person chosen reports to any other attending.

Before scheduling the meetings the deputy manager contacts the manager or supervisor of each person to be invited. He explains that the purpose is to help John Mortimer learn direct from employees what they think should be done to improve the company's performance so that it can become the sort of firm they have been hearing he wants to create. It is stressed that anyone attending the meeting will be talking 'off the record' – no direct actions will stem from these meetings relating to the individual employee or his immediate line manager.

The initial meetings prove difficult to establish as there is suspicion that the exercise is useless. Some managers and supervisors resent their staff being asked to a strange meeting with the general manager, without them attending too. The deputy manager uncovers another worry of middle managers and supervisors, a concern that subordinates involved in the meetings will be leaving tasks that are equally or more important.

Resentment and distrust make John Mortimer realize that he must spend more time discussing, presenting and gaining commitment to the project. To achieve this he creates a small project team of managers drawn from across the whole spectrum of the firm. The deputy general manager is made responsible for ensuring that ideas flowing from the Sensing exercise are followed through, underlining top management's commitment to the process. This begins to build confidence that it will be more than a talking shop.

Meetings of the project team with the general manager confirm and disseminate the message that he is genuinely interested in learning what people are thinking. This knowledge permeates the organization more effectively than announcements, memos or newsletters. An important task which the project team achieves is clarifying that the Sensing groups are non-negotiable, ie those invited must attend.

The project team helps the general manager and his deputy rethink how people will be selected – on a random basis – the mechanics of inviting around 120 people, the structure of the meetings, what questions will be asked, how the information will be handled and so on. The location for the meeting is carefully chosen. The general manager's office is too daunting, even another manager's office is considered unsuitable. The only other meeting rooms are too small, so the staff restaurant is adapted with screens sectioning off an area making a pleasant, informal setting.

Each meeting starts with a warm up by the deputy manager, who again clarifies its purpose, explaining that the general manager will arrive in about half an hour. The whole event will be open and informal and he suggests a way of treating the occasion:

'Imagine that you were on a train going to visit relatives and you happen to find yourself sitting next to the general manager. He's obviously in a mood to hear how you see things in the company at present; over a beer or a coffee you take the opportunity of telling him!'

To emphasize the informality beer, sandwiches and coffee are provided and to create an open style of meeting the chairs are arranged in a circle, rather than around a table.

Confidentiality is also discussed. The deputy manager confirms that no actions will result from these meetings relating to individuals, their immediate line manager or supervisor. Information will only be used in summary form, not with named people's contributions. The deputy also indicates that he proposes to use a tape recorder to simplify note taking. The general manager may also use the tapes later to refresh his memory or to present word pictures to the division's top staff. If any member of the group prefers he will immediately stop the tape now, or at any time during the meeting.

A review of Sensing by the project team has shown the importance of not attempting too much at each session. To prompt people to think about the issues they might want to raise, the deputy manager shows a flip chart with some appropriate prompts:

- The three things I really dislike about working here are . . .

- I really like working here because . . .

- The main ways I'd like to improve things around here are . . .

He reminds them that these are only prompts and anyone can raise anything they feel strongly about.

Although John Mortimer is forceful and self confident he is worried that people will close up and not talk frankly. At the suggestion of the project team he comes armed with a few direct questions if the meeting flags. These do not deal with general issues such as: 'How can we make our firm the best in the field?', or 'How can we improve our export performance?' about which the participants may lack knowledge. Instead they are specific and allow people to use their personal experience:

- What sort of things seem to prevent you doing your job even better?

- If you had to describe in one word the present management way of helping you do a better job what would it be?

- Do you get enough information to do your job well?

- What sort of things would make this an exciting, attractive place to work in each day?

Most of the people at the meeting do not know each other or only slightly, but by the time the general manager arrives they are relaxed and chatting about the issues on the flip chart. When John Mortimer sits down there is a momentary awkward silence. The conversation starts again when he smiles, helps himself to a beer and sits back looking interested. Any anxiety that he might not obtain honest opinions is quickly dispelled. What people say is usually straight from the shoulder, often insightful to a point that surprises him. In every group there are always one or two people who moan and an even greater number who clearly have something to 'get off their chest'. Mostly though everyone is constructive, committed to the spirit of the Sensing meeting.

A common theme that emerges in all the meetings is concern that all this talking may not lead to any changes. Certainly the Sensing meeting is ripe for abuse, with managers collecting quantities of information only to sink into the daily grind of keeping the organization going, maintaining the *status quo*. When pressed on this John Mortimer refers to the role of the deputy director who chairs the project team and confirms that there is now a task force for seeing that what emerges is turned into an action programme.

After each meeting a letter from the general manager goes to the participants thanking them for their contribution and explaining that the entire Sensing exercise will be completed within two months. There will then be a four-week period of analysis followed by a review of the results by top management. Specific action is expected to start a month later. The participants also receive a brief summary of the points raised in their particular meeting without mentioning anyone's name.

The meetings with John Mortimer are spread over two months by which time both he and the deputy director possess a huge amount of data. They are also extremely tired. Sensing is no easy option, being emotionally and physically draining, particularly if you must always appear alert and interested in what is being said.

Data analysis is handled in several ways:

- Content analysis

- Impression reports by the general manager and his deputy

- Analysis by type of group.

The project team undertakes the first and last of these tasks, using tape transcripts plus the tapes themselves. The reports of the two senior managers are based on their own impressions of the meetings using their memory, notes and occasionally the tapes. Their two reports are submitted to the project team.

The project team prepares a presentation to the board of directors and a second for other groups of managers. The presentation shows the main findings using facts and interpretation, combined with actual play-backs of selected comments from the groups. The presentation is hard hitting, specific and at times amusing, as extracts from the tapes bring colour to the points being made.

Three meetings are held to inform those who attended the original Sensing meetings about the management response and this gives participants a chance to hear about likely actions. A company newsletter is sent to every employee explaining the results and a regular bulletin is issued on how the management is following through on the findings.

Although the results of the Sensing exercise take time to permeate the whole organization everyone is soon aware of what has emerged from the meetings, together with a provisional list of proposed actions. The latter have been hammered out in the board room where the top team has been confronting the more uncomfortable messages emerging from the meetings. The selected tape play-backs make an eloquent and powerful case for long-due changes, particularly relating to management style and communications.

From John Mortimer's viewpoint he has achieved some important results from in his change effort which are shown in Box 34.

Box 34

Results from a Sensing exercise

- Hard data available about what changes are needed

- How to tackle change becomes clearer

- Senior management team and below more aware of the need to make changes

- A significant and committed core of people created who 'own' the need for changes and want to see them through

- Significant number of employees at all levels enabled to speak their minds about what changes are required

- Creative and new ideas identified to form an agenda for a longer term change effort

- Programme of management action identified and initiated

Variations

There are many variations of Sensing. It can be done on a one-to-one basis rather than in a group, and with more structured questions than used in the above example. The advantage of a group session is being able to test whether the ideas, perceptions and issues raised are commonly held. Occasionally, as with John Mortimer and his deputy, it makes sense for more than one senior person to attend, to compare notes and to watch for misunderstandings.

Sensing interviews, and even group sessions can be conducted on the telephone. The latter prevents important non-verbal communication and is less effective than being face to face. It is also feasible, though costly, to use television conference technology to save people travelling to a particular location.

Though part of the power of Sensing is that management is actually seen to be listening, it is possible to use a consultant to conduct sensing meetings. When this happens there is a risk that people will dismiss the whole exercise as a charade. However, a mixture of consultant and management-led sensing groups may prove effective. A consultant may also be able to extract more honest opinions from staff in some organizations where managers have a poor record of listening to staff views.

Finally Sensing may be spread over years rather than weeks or months. In 1980 in the American Zebco company that specialized in making fishing reels, the vice president of manufacturing started having two-hour meetings with employees in groups of four. He explained about the need to improve quality and the need for lower costs, and in additional plant meetings he asked what people needed to do their job better. It took two years for the vice president to meet all the employees.

Questions

The use of direct questions in Sensing has to be considered carefully. It may prove overwhelming and rapport needs to be established before presenting direct questions to groups. The sequence of questions should be adapted to the local situation. A basic structure for helping to formulate questions is shown in Box 35.

Devising questions for Sensing meetings is relatively easy. The skill is to use them sparingly, without creating communication blocks or causing people to withhold. The phrasing of the questions as well as their delivery should be non-threatening and it is also worth checking that each question is fully understood (see also Chapter 20 on Verbal Skills).

Box 35

Structure for formulating Sensing questions

- ROLES – for example, what do you do, what are your responsibilities; how would you describe your job to someone else; are you clear how you fit into the organization?

- GOALS – for example, what are your short term goals for your job right now; what should the organization do to help you achieve these goals; do you have any long term career goals; what work would you like to be doing next in this organization?

- YOUR JOB – for example, what are the good things and the bad things about your job; what parts of the job seem important to you; what parts of your job seem a waste of time; what extra responsibility might you have which you do not have now; is there anything you do that should be done by someone else; to do your job well do you feel well supported and informed by managers?

- ORGANIZATION – for example, what is it about this organization which helps you to be effective; what things around here make you less than fully effective; why is it worth coming to work here; why do people stay here for many years; why do people leave?

- RELATIONSHIPS – for example, how would you describe your relationship with your immediate boss, and with the person above the boss; what are their respective strengths and weaknesses; what kind of relations do you have with people at your same level in the organization; how would you describe these people; what kind of subordinates do you have and how effective are your relationships with them?

- YOUR TEAM – for example, what are the major problems facing your work team right now; how are decisions made in your team; how supportive is your team when you have a problem; does your team regularly review its effectiveness, and what it is trying to achieve?

- CHANGES – for example, what changes should your immediate boss make right now; what changes should the senior management make; what should change in your team; in what way would you like to see those who report direct to you change; what changes should you be making right now?

- HERE AND NOW – what do you think about this meeting, interview, discussion etc; what do you think about the organizer of this meeting; what do you think the organizer of the meeting is feeling or thinking; what do you feel about the person holding this meeting?

The pros and cons

Some of the benefits from Sensing were revealed when John Mortimer used it (see above). The more general pros and cons are summarized in Box 36. It has an immediate appeal for some managers and in an adapted form is used by many consultants. It demands a significant commitment of time and resourses.

Box 36

Pros and cons of Sensing

PROS	CONS
UNDERSTANDING – a chance to check out what people feel and say	EXPENSE – demanding of time, space and staff; can be more economical than individual interviews
AMPLIFICATION – comments can be elaborated and expanded	
	GOALS – goals not always shared or understood
DISCOVERY – unknown problems can be uncovered	
	ANALYSIS – data can be difficult and time consuming to analyse or summarize; data may be lost in the vast amount of information generated
SUPPLEMENTING – can support and supplement data gathered from other sources	
LANGUAGE – is that of the participant not the manager; makes the results more acceptable	THREAT – anxiety-creating for some participants; unless understood by line managers can be resisted strongly; usefulness limited if lack of trust exists between individuals at different levels in the organization; some people may feel they are being spied on
CREDIBILITY – data gathered this way is often more credible than through other means	
CONTACT – provides an opportunity for personal contact between change agent and others	
	ACCESS – requires people to be brought together who may be spread across different locations
OPENNESS – when people feel they are being understood they are more open	
RAPPORT – easier than some other methods to establish rapport between participants and manager, hence more openness and useful information gained	

Effective though Sensing may be, it is only one of many diagnostic change techniques. It cannot replace ordinary communication channels, nor is it suitable for judging or reprimanding employees or as a platform for promoting senior management's views. It should be chosen because it answers a particular management need to learn what changes are needed now.

GUIDELINES

- SPEND time discussing, presenting and gaining commitment to the Sensing project

- ENSURE sufficient time and resources to conduct the exercise

- BUILD confidence that the exercise will be more than a talking shop

- CLARIFY that attendance at the Sensing group is non-negotiable

- DECIDE whether people will be selected from vertical or horizontal slices of the organization

- DETERMINE the mechanics of: inviting people, meeting structure, questions to be asked, how information will be handled, location and so on

- SET limited objectives for each session

- PROMOTE a relaxed, informal atmosphere in Sensing sessions

- CONFIRM that named individual contributions are confidential and not disseminated

- OFFER to switch off tape recorders if requested

- GIVE each Sensing group warm up issues to discuss

- SEND written thanks to participants; confirm when the total exercise will end; state when action will start

- PROVIDE participants with a brief summary of their own or group's contribution

- ANALYSE both content and impressions from the Sensing meetings

- PRESENT findings to relevant power groups in the organization.

Techniques
17. Mundane tools of change

The note was short and to the point. 'When do I get your report on the export quota system?' It was a tickler, a reminder that action was expected. The person on the receiving end knew that his boss was becoming impatient, wanting results.

Ticklers follow up outstanding tasks, usually arriving at increasingly short intervals until the recipient delivers. Sometimes the system is computerized so that until you cancel the instruction a reminder comes with inexorable regularity. Anyone who has delayed paying a gas or electricity bill knows how the tickler system works, often accompanied with dire warnings about what will happen if you do not act.

Ticklers are one of many mundane tools of day-to-day change. They are inextricably linked to the daily occurrences that fill a manager's diary. They are not concerned with the more strategic aspects of organizational change. Every manager develops a personal set of mundane tools for making things happen. Some of these tools reflect one's personality, for example a frequent use of flip charts and verbal presentations. Others are the nuts and bolts of being organized, such as daily 'to do' lists.

Large scale organizational change ultimately reduces to small and often simple tasks that somebody somewhere must perform. Because mundane tools are so basic their power and connection with the larger change effort are seldom appreciated. They oil the wheels of change rather than turn them.

According to consultant Tom Peters, who identified the idea of mundane tools some years ago, there are:

- Symbolic activities

- Patterns or grouping of activities

- Interactive settings.

We can also add a fourth which cuts across these and which can be called Task Improvers.

Symbolic activities

These activities signal what the manager thinks, conveying vision, goals and values. They stand for something that matters. By itself an individual activity may have little meaning, cumulatively many of them amount to a clear message.

Examples of symbols include reports, agendas, physical settings, public statements and so on. When a manager ensures that his diary is booked for a regular budget review this is a practical and also symbolic message. At both Ford and Chrysler Lee Iacocca, the American car chief, tried to get the people who worked for him to use a quarterly review system. It was how he controlled things, always adding: 'I'm not saying you have to do it my way. But if you don't, you'd better find something else that produces the same results'. By committing himself to that particular task Iacocca ensured that time for it was always planned. This was noted by other people and modelling their actions on his behaviour others were able to draw certain conclusions. His commitment helped shape the climate which Iacocca wanted to create.

Similarly the regular two monthly presentation of Nielsen market share ratings in Pepsi Cola became a symbol – beating the one competitor that mattered: Coca Cola. Gathering to hear the presentations Pepsi managers knew that careers rode on swings of a fraction in share points. A one point shift translated into sales worth millions of dollars.

The use of agendas to control and influence expectations is another example of how symbolic activities play an important role in affection change. While it matters what goes onto the agenda, equally significant is what is omitted, as this too can colour people's thinking and priorities. The kind of questions which a manager asks can also directly and symbolically point to what matters.

The setting in which meetings are held can symbolize a style or attitude. For instance, when John Roberts became managing director of a medium sized publishing company he seldom talked to subordinates in his office from behind a desk. Instead he installed some easy chairs and discussed business sitting in comfortable seats. This was in contrast to his predecessor who stayed defended behind his desk. Roberts used the symbolism of the physical setting to send a strong message that he was relaxed, approachable and cared more about the subject matter than status or appearance. The locations in which a manager is seen or not seen, personal contacts and how personal staff are used may also symbolize a management message.

Symbolism can be converted into a stunning but practical tool. When General Electric was experiencing massive quality control problems the production manager installed traffic lights in the factory which turned red each time quality fell below acceptable levels. Assembly lines shut down until corrective action was taken.

Patterns or grouping of activities

Relatively low key management activities may form trends which, over time, influence large numbers of people. There are usually obvious groupings of these particular mundane tools of change. Giving positive reinforcement, behaving in a particularly consistent way, tending towards action instead of analysis, are all examples of how managers use quite small measures to focus on change.

A manager may, for example, develop a particularly effective way of reinforcing activities which are to be encouraged. This might be through the use of praise and paying more attention to successes than failure.

One of the best tools is based on the idea of many small successes. You establish a pattern of frequent and consistent small successes rather than a single large achievement. It may not be immediately obvious how some small successes contribute to the overall change effort. A climate is gradually created in which the manager's actions are increasingly seen as credible. Building on small successes takes patience and is rather like doing a jigsaw. Consistent small successes shape people's expectations. In raising an organization's profile, for example, change is influenced by many activities, not by a single once-only event.

Interactive setting

Organizations are basically groups of people with common goals. Tools that affect how people interact can be useful for effecting change. Examples of the use of settings include modelling to influence others, location of meetings, agenda control, questioning approaches, use of deadlines, use of minutes and so on.

A company wanting to improve its environmental record might establish a special project group with members from outside environmental agencies. The new interactive setting may become influential in affecting future decisions of the organization.

Similarly, in a London local authority social services department problems arose in ensuring that local health and social services worked closely together to provide an integrated service. After studying the problem the solution adopted was the creation of local forums in which specialists from the various different services could meet to solve joint problems. The new interactive setting improved the use of scarce resources.

The choice of meeting place is another interactive tool. Where you meet subordinates or your boss can influence the nature of interactions between you. Some senior managers, for instance, never visit subordinates' offices for a meeting, even a casual one, expecting all interactions to take place in their own office. While this may underline the senior manager's power it may also widen the communication gap.

Control over agendas has long been recognized as a useful, mundane tool. Deciding what will be discussed influences the nature of the interaction; giving high priority to a topic signals new approaches and directions. The structure and presentation of issues can also have a significant impact. For example, a manager who insists that there should be a detailed three-year plan of development for a particular service or product may be initiating a whole sequence of events in which people have to create this plan.

Requiring that reports are based on well presented facts and arguments, with collaboration by all those who can contribute, is another interactive device. This occurs for instance when a personnel director insists that all major reports should mention any implications for equal opportunities in the organization.

Task Improvers

Task Improvers are the mass of small scale management techniques which contribute to a manager's overall effectiveness. They impinge indirectly on achieving change. Probably the most widely used task improver is the Action List containing priority tasks with which the manager is currently concerned and which may be ranked or categorized in some useful way.

Used by successful managers the world over, action lists are a combination of reminders to do certain things and an aid for handling your time. They are usually updated weekly and, if necessary, daily. Sometimes they are kept on a computer so that a fresh copy can be produced whenever the list changes. Some people also categorize each item on their list in relation to its importance and urgency. A simple way of sorting out the tasks is shown in Chart 24.

The discipline of the action list is used by determined managers to create clear goals for themselves. Lee Iacocca, President of Chrysler, usually finished his week by preparing a list for the following one which was headed:

The things I will achieve next week are: . . .

Chart 24

Prioritising your time

		URGENCY	
		HIGH	LOW
IMPORTANCE	HIGH	DO IT NOW! DO IT YOURSELF	DO IT – LATER
	LOW	ASK SOMEONE ELSE TO DO IT	DON'T DO IT!

In connection with change, regular supervisory meetings with subordinates is another Task Improver which influences other people's priorities. Supervisory meetings need to occur at least monthly and in some cases weekly. Their relevance to the change effort is that they provide a framework for reviewing work in hand and a forum for dealing with issues that have aroused strong feelings.

Another Task Improver is to analyse how you are spending your time so as to focus your efforts on major change activity, instead of becoming immersed in paperwork. Keeping a log for a couple of weeks, in which you note and analyse your use of time, can be helpful. You can adapt the Stress Log shown on page 134 for this purpose.

A much used Task Improver is to evolve a way of handling constant interruptions so that you are not always breaking off to do something else. Research on successful change shows that it is the intensity of obsession by managers who want to make things happen which counts. Frequent interruptions prevent a focussed effort from developing. Consider, for instance, selecting a period during the day when you will only be available for real emergencies. Perhaps put a sign on your door saying 'engaged' and insist that people respect it. Think hard about why you seem to have so many interruptions. Be honest, maybe you enjoy them too much!

GUIDELINES

● USE the mundane tools to underpin your change effort

● ADOPT symbolic activities to convey messages about vision and values, including for example commitment to certain regular tasks, settings for meeting places, use of agendas etc

● LOOK for activities which can form trends and that influence large numbers of people, for example use of praise, a flow of small successes etc

● INFLUENCE the settings in which inter-actions between people or different groups can occur

● BUILD your own collection of simple task improvers such as action lists, regular supervision of subordinates, team meetings, time management and so on.

Techniques
18. Management by walking about

Robert McNamara, at one time in control of part of the Ford Motor Company, was convinced that a certain new model should show a particular level of fuel consumption. However the results varied from one test to another.

The man in charge of the tests kept sending McNamara the figures, explaining that there were always variations in wind conditions, drivers and the cars themselves. McNamara was insistent. He had graphs and charts and he felt that the numbers simply must behave.

It was another Ford man who came to the rescue. He suggested to the man in charge of the tests: 'Why don't you do the testing and then when it's done I'll go in a corner and smooth the numbers a little'. The numbers were smoothed and brought to McNamara who never went near the actual cars himself. McNamara beamed – the car was shown to be performing according to his numbers.

McNamara should have seen for himself what was happening. Since he disliked cars and was not too keen on meeting the people in the front line who were doing the actual work, he stayed tied to his desk, trying to control by numbers.

The importance of staying in close touch by walking around and seeing for yourself sounds so basic as to be hardly worth mentioning. Yet it is often neglected as a way of managing. Getting out and about is given all sorts of names: walking the shop floor, staying in touch, keeping a management profile, and even MBWA – Management by Walking, or Wandering, About. Contrary to an increasingly popular myth Peters and Waterman were not the ones to discover it, although in their study of *Excellence* they drew attention to its importance, finding that it was a pillar by which the highly successful Hewlett Packard computer firm operated. Nor is there any secret to it, though many managers seem reluctant either to do it or acknowledge its value.

At the tail end of many a large organizational dinosaur employees will often describe the lack of MBWA:

183

'The top brass? We never see them here'
'Our head of department? Never comes near us'
'Now you mention it, I've never even met the person in charge'
'She visits alright, spends most of her time in the office
   with our supervisor'
'Only time I've met the top boss was when I joined'.

These comments are rarer where managing change is valued and managers at all levels get out and about, staying in touch with what is, or is not happening. No matter how senior you become there is no substitute for MBWA.

In one highly profitable US confectionery firm the head office appointed the managing director of the UK subsidiary at a salary far above the normal market rate. Before leaving for England for his new job he received a message from head office: 'Good luck! Ask for help anytime, but if there's a strike you're fired.' That MD soon acquired an obsession with staying in touch, leaving his desk, plunging into the factory, and visiting all the distribution points. He demanded such close contact with trade union representatives that he insisted on meeting them before they sought him out. By his walkabout approach he anticipated strikes, go slows and overtime bans. He was so in touch that he could smell trouble coming.

Management by walking about is seeing and talking to employees at all levels, learning what they are thinking, tapping their ideas and enthusiasm. The larger the organization, the more important this task becomes, especially for those in the rarified atmosphere of the boardroom. A rather wider view of MBWA is getting out amongst customers, suppliers, competitors, politicians, almost anyone outside the hierarchy.

Senior managers can spend their lives driving a desk, answering phone calls, handling colleagues' questions, ploughing through reading matter and being legitimately busy. Once in such a groove it requires a special effort to develop time for walkabouts.

Resist the tendency to become almost totally reliant on talking to your immediate peers. While they have plenty in common with you and are usually sympathetic to your problems, such a narrow focus is apt to create management stagnation rather than the drive to promote change or learn whether agreed changes are actually happening.

How much in touch do you have to be? This is a dilemma as you ascend the corporate tree. Spend too little time walking about and you may be unpleasantly surprised by events. Spend too much time and you risk being forgotten by those at the centre. Staying in touch with all parts of your organization develops your authority and prestige and being well informed makes you valuable:

**The bigger your job the more important it is to
meet all levels of employees at their work place.**

Penetrating the structure

Managing by walking about helps reduce the stifling effects of the organization's formal structure. While the latter allows work to be organized and clarifies relationships between different employees, it also creates communication barriers. Walkabouts also reduce the isolation between senior and junior employees, between one section or unit and another, as you pass through sharing news, ideas and encouragement.

When there is serious trouble you need to be sure that you will be told about it and if necessary called in. Walkabouts guarantee that you are seldom far from some contact who can lead you to where your management input is required. From regular walkabouts you learn to sniff out the need for change. Seeing many different situations enables you to use your brain's computer-like ability to spot patterns and make new connections. You will often see opportunities which other people, apparently closer to the situation, have missed.

Walkabouts have a significant impact on employee morale and productivity. Evidence from the famous Hawthorne experiments, for example, suggested that it may be less important what managers do than that they are perceived to be trying to improve work situations.

By your presence at local work places you can actively encourage experiments, the generation of ideas and perhaps most important the habit of critical self appraisal. This does not happen automatically since much depends on your personal style and approach. A manager who arrives and immediately starts being highly critical would be wasting the power of MBWA. Once people who work for you know that you are genuinely interested in their contribution, you will seldom be short of vital information on ways to achieve better results.

A less obvious benefit from an MBWA style is that you are in a continuous learning situation. The stimulus should prevent you from becoming jaded or bored with your job. As many managers have discovered, walkabouts are fun.

Using MBWA you will find ways to reinforce change. For example, in one public service agency a senior manager launched a campaign to improve sickness rates. He visited several outposted staff locations with a vital piece of paper in his pocket. It contained a list of people who had just completed two years continuous service without a day's sick leave and he made a special point of personally congratulating them.

Behind many change efforts lies the need to introduce new value systems and influence norms. Using MBWA managers can talk to a wide range of employees about 'what we are trying to do', and explain that 'what really matters is . . .'

How is it done?

'When I just wander round I'm not sure what to do or say' is how one anxious manager initially responded to the experience of building MBWA into his timetable. There are various ways of making it a rewarding experience. The most basic is being willing to listen, leaving space for people to talk to you, to share their feelings about what is happening. This is as important as your own message of change or new values. Stay quiet, smile and look interested and you will usually provoke a steady flow of news, views and useful information. In the American Sperry company, for example, the importance of listening has become a company obsession and hundreds of managers have been trained to do it better. On walkabouts keep your ration of talking to listening at around 20:70 (see also Chapter 20 on Verbal Skills).

Focus your approach by selecting something highly specific to review during the MBWA. Just as scanning pages of print becomes easier if you are hunting for a particular fact or name, so with walkabouts a useful device is seeking specific kinds of information. This might include signs that employees are genuinely enjoying their work, or at worst are not bored by it. For example, do employees seem to smile and catch your eye? Is there evidence that people are experimenting and testing out new ideas? One manager asked 'What's new?' so often that when he arrived people began beating him to it by asking him 'What's new?' Still, they realized that he valued change and wanted to hear about people trying new ways of doing things.

Develop a list of topic areas to check on regularly. A useful framework for formulating your search is the one presented in Box 37. The headings suggest various lines of enquiry to take during walkabouts.

If you work in a mainly hierarchical organization it makes sense to meet employees in groups or teams, sometimes with their supervisor present and occasionally alone. If you meet them without their immediate boss present, make it clear to all concerned that

Box 37

Check points for walkabouts

- *Leadership*: is there someone in this role at each level who keeps potential trouble spots under control; how effective is this leadership, is it working well or badly?

- *Purposes*: employees must know what business they are in; do people really understand the aims and values of the organization?

- *Structure:* how is work organized, is workload divided evenly?

- *Helpful mechanisms*: are there effective devices for enabling different parts of the organization to work well together?

- *Relationships*: competing technologies and conflict between individuals must be managed well, is this happening?

- *Incentives*: is there encouragement for doing all that needs to be done?

---

you will not be issuing any direct or indirect orders and this will avoid undermining the line manager's authority. You are there merely to encourage people to open up and talk about things that may sometimes be hard to share with their immediate supervisor. Request the meetings you need, rather than arrive out of the blue. This will ensure that you do not disrupt other people's work too much except on a planned basis (see also Chapter 16 on Sensing).

MBWA is a demanding experience. When you come face to face with those on the receiving end of change they may unload on you some of the stresses they are experiencing. It is important therefore to:

Know your facts about the change and explain the benefits clearly.

Another peg on which to hang MBWA visits and find pointers for discussions and enquiries is your organization's philosophy or mission statement with which everyone can readily identify. Bob Haas, the president and chief executive of Levi Strauss, the highly successful jeans and clothes concern, defined his company's philosophy as a set of goals relating to people, customers, the stores where clothes are sold and so on. For example, where people are concerned the philosophy states:

Create a small company environment; establish a climate of

openness; encourage risk taking; provide a safe, wholesome working environment that is stimulating, pleasant and supports maximum personal effectiveness.

Strauss executives on MBWA have a common view of what they expect to find and can test reality against expectations.

A possible drawback of MBWA is that people may see you as inspecting them, searching for things which they are doing wrong. You can avoid giving this impression by keeping your critical comments to a minimum and by not asking too many direct questions. Invite individuals to tell you what they are doing at that moment and to explain what they think about it. One manager, for example, who visited a work location stopped to look at some complicated forms a clerk was completing. The clerk explained what she did and while the manager stayed silent and interested, she proceeded to wonder aloud why the forms were not handled on a computer. The manager wondered too and later installed a small computer system which released the clerk's time for more useful and interesting work.

Maintain a regular MBWA style by planning the visits in your diary several weeks or months ahead. If you rely on snatching the occasional half day you will soon be stuck behind a desk again. Tell people that you want to be invited when they have something new or interesting they would like to share. This way the onus is not entirely on you to persist with MBWA. As a prompt regularly review the check questions shown in Box 38. If you have junior managers or supervisors reporting to you it is worth posing these to them too.

Box 38

MBWA questions

- What work locations have been visited in the last two weeks?

- What was done to demonstrate or communicate the organization's main mission(s) or central values?

- Outside of immediate working colleagues who have you/I talked to and what was learned?

- What recognition was offered for work done or successes?

- What action has been or will be taken as a result of the last visit?

- Will any successes or good practices be communicated elsewhere and if so how?

GUIDELINES

- CHANGE your timetable so that walkabouts happen regularly

- FOCUS on specifics during the MBWA

- KNOW your facts about the change situation and be able to explain the benefits

- MEET employees in groups or teams, sometimes with their supervisor present and occasionally alone

- LISTEN! keep your talking to hearing ratio at 20:70

- AVOID criticism, if you must criticize do it simply

- ENQUIRE what individuals are doing right now, encourage them to explain what they think about it

- LET people know that you want to be asked to visit when they have something new, interesting or particular problems they would like to share

- AVOID too many direct questions

- LOOK for activities to praise

- SEEK news of activities designed to increase productivity, develop communications, do things better and so on

- ENQUIRE about failures, show that responsible attempts to improve things will be encouraged

- AVOID giving orders directly to subordinates of managers below you

- NEVER reprimand someone in front of other people.

Techniques
19. Team building

When Malcolm Payne became responsible for a newly formed division in a large international travel agency he found many of the services provided were of low quality and unco-ordinated, and staff morale was poor. His major change action was a restructuring which he introduced in the first few months. This clarified lines of accountability, reduced spans of control and created new lines of communication.

After meeting all the managers for whom he was responsible Malcolm realized that to restructure effectively required more than just rearranging the pieces of the organizational jigsaw. There had to be new ways of working; new formal relationships had to be reinforced; and, above all, people had to learn to work together in a more concerted way. What was needed was team building.

All managers and supervisors met for a day to review how to use teamwork to build on the changes already made. Obstacles to effective teams were reviewed and ways of eliminating them identified. The various teams were encouraged to take one or more days away from the workplace to review their effectiveness and goals in relation to the division's overall objectives. Senior managers were available to help at the sessions, and in certain teams which required a considerable amount of help an outside organizational consultant was used.

These team sessions reduced hidden resentment about the recent reorganization and began harnessing people's creative energies. Teams were asked to set specific aims for the coming months and in this way members began experiencing shared goals. Regular team building sessions became a legitimate activity in which managers and staff could invest their time. From these stemmed many of the improvements envisaged at the start of the reorganization.

Organizations which are totally committed to coping with change realize the importance of teamwork. They convert the negative backbiting behaviour usually associated with 'politics' into something positive by emphasizing teamwork. Looking at Morgan Bank, Bankers Trust, IBM and Olivetti in Italy, consultant Robert

Waterman Jr asked: 'Where is the frenzy? The fervour? The angst? Don't these people watch television and know that life is supposed to be frantic . . . How can they be so calm yet do so well in today's "fast paced, split-second, rate-of-change-was-never-greater" world? The answer is teamwork, which starts at the top.'

Effective teamwork seldom happens by chance or luck. It stems from sound leadership and the use of principles which any change minded manager can use.

Harder than it looks

There is an important distinction between working in teams and team building. Although many managers are responsible for teams they are not always committed to any investment in team building. While supporting the idea of teams some people assume that the team building process occurs naturally. It can do, particularly if the group is facing intense pressure or stress. But actively building a team offers a more systematic way of speeding up the cohesion of the group, which can otherwise take months or years to achieve.

As a way of achieving organizational change team building is increasingly being given a high priority. In contrast, some people believe that it is the efforts of individuals that really count in making things happen. Teams may also be judged to be irrelevant for dealing with many of the major issues currently concerning the organization, which itself may not see organizational change as a key issue.

For anyone committed to team building as a way of achieving change it can be frustrating that not everyone embraces this approach. When pressed by an enthusiastic colleague to pursue team building one manager retorted: 'You're proselytizing. Well it's not a sect that I want to join.' His reaction reflects how many people feel when faced with team building enthusiasts. If a group of people must work together regularly it does not automatically follow that they should function like a team with common goals, mutual respect and shared values.

Another objection to team building as a way of achieving organizational change is that it simply takes too long. However, most major worthwhile organizational changes also take a long time so that team building is seldom a waste of time.

Organizations which cope well with change are usually those where the importance of relationships between groups and individuals is acknowledged and there is an emphasis on interdependence and shared responsibility. This requires an openness, a willingness to confront issues and individuals and a recognition that the efforts of a group can often be more effective than the same number of people working separately. In handling change, therefore, managers need skills which encourage the inter-disciplinary approach, particularly for tackling difficult or complex situations such as creating a corporate strategy.

Influencing how groups interact with each other has been widely used as a way both to generate and to respond to change. In recent years there has also been a growing awareness of the importance of helping individuals transcend their team role in the interest of developing themselves and the enterprise. Team building is thus no panacea, but when it is used selectively, it can:

- Create a climate of social support for a particular change

- Open up the communication processes

- Encourage creative problem solving

- Obtain commitment to decisions

- Assist in achieving individual and organizational goals

- Foster interdependence and group effort.

Making a start

How do you build a successful, change minded team? The first step is to identify the group of people who you think should be working as a team. Try defining:

Why should this group of people work as a team?

To do this answer the questions shown in Box 39. The answers can usefully involve the group of people themselves in thinking about the two main issues:

Are we a team?

Should we work at becoming a (better) team?

To start team building you may wish to use a training specialist or a consultant with relevant experience. Alternatively you can lead the team building yourself using do-it-yourself guides such as those listed in the further reading section at the end of this book. You may also decide that you want some training on team building

Box 39

Deciding if a group is a team

- Do people have more things in common than differences – YES/NO

- Are there complex issues which are better tackled using many people's ideas and skills – YES/NO

- Can someone be identified as a team leader, manager or 'chairman' with a role to promote teamwork – YES/NO

- Are the individuals willing to work together more closely – YES/NO

- Is it practical in terms of time, travel distances and other constraints for this group to meet regularly to work both formally as a team and on the process of team building – YES/NO

If the answer is NO to any of these questions, team building is likely to be inappropriate.

methods and there are many courses available on this subject.

Whoever organizes the process should see that the group takes time away from daily work pressures to concentrate on specific team building tasks. These may be a mixture of working on issues facing the group and particularly techniques that promote teamwork.

Forcing the group to do something exceptionally challenging is another, somewhat controversial way of speeding up the team building process. The latter must involve activities designed to help the individuals get to know each other better, finding out each other's strengths and weaknesses, and learning to trust each other. One British managing director took his entire top team, including their wives, to climb the highest mountain in Central Africa. This proved a life-changing experience for all concerned and they returned to form a work group with tremendous cohesion and trust.

Team roles

Are you a shaper or a company worker? Or is finishing your preference? Perhaps you see yourself mainly as a team worker or someone who likes monitoring and evaluating? If none of these, how about being chairman? Roles like these make or break a management team. Omit one and the team may never rise above the average.

One of the most thorough investigations undertaken to unravel why management teams succeed or fail was by Meredith Belbin who studied hundreds of teams and thousands of managers. His results are often used to improve a team's functioning. People play eight main roles in management teams. Each has some positive features and some weaknesses. Successful teams are a mixture of people whose skills complement each other (see Box 40).

Belbin had enviable opportunities to create entirely new teams, experimenting until he found the right recipe. Few managers in real life, even those determined to shake up the entire organization, have the chance to start with a blank sheet and devise the ideal team. Most managers inherit their teams or part of them and must use the available skills to obtain the best results.

To prepare the team for looking at roles the members first read Belbin's book on *Team Management*, or a lengthy summary of it. Each person then completes a simple questionnaire from which is produced a team and an individual profile. These show the leanings each person has towards the eight roles and what kind of mix of roles exists in the team as a whole.

As an individual you learn your role preferences which can be compared to those of your colleagues. The profiles provide the starting point for considering how the team can begin functioning better. They can also uncover why the team occasionally wastes time, handling some tasks inefficiently.

Although individuals may emerge as being strong in one particular role this does not mean that they must always play this role. They may be only slightly less powerful in another role which is badly needed in the particular team. The assumption behind the role mixture is that successful teams contain at least one person able to play each of the eight roles. The team should accept the importance of each role as contributing equally towards collective success. Another assumption is that people can switch roles.

Superficially Shaper and Chairman seem to be the prestige roles, the ones for which highly competitive members of the team may fight. In practice, however, these roles are only successful in combination with others. For instance, a team with too many Shapers may undervalue the person who regularly reminds the team that it must complete its task – Completer/Finisher. Similarly, a team full of aspiring Chairmen may spend time fighting for the leadership while devaluing someone who is good at providing information on which the team can make choices – Resources Investigator.

Once the team realizes how its profile affects performance it becomes easier to change the situation. For example, a public services agency team working on the Belbin analysis found that it was short of Finishers. The team tended to assume that once a decision was made action would automatically happen. Follow

Box 40

Useful people to have in teams

Team worker	Typical features	Positive qualities	Allowable weaknesses
Company worker	Conservative, dutiful, predictable	Organizing ability, practical common sense, hard-working, self-discipline	Lack of flexibility, unresponsiveness to unproven ideas
Chairman	Calm, self-confident, controlled	A capacity for treating and welcoming all potential contributors on their merits and without prejudice. A strong sense of objectives	No more than ordinary in terms of intellect or creative ability
Shaper	Highly strung, outgoing, dynamic	Drive and a readiness to challenge inertia, ineffectiveness, complacency or self-deception	Prone to provocation, irritation and impatience
Plant	Individualistic, serious-minded, unorthodox	Genius, imagination, intellect, knowledge	Up in the clouds, inclined to disregard practical details or protocol
Resources investigator	Extrovert, enthusiastic, curious, communicative	A capacity for contacting people and exploring anything new. An ability to respond to challenge	Liable to lose interest once the initial fascination has passed
Monitor-evaluator	Sober, unemotional, prudent	Judgement, discretion, hard-headedness	Lacks inspiration or the ability to motivate others
Team worker	Socially orientated, rather mild, sensitive	An ability to respond to people and to situations, and to promote team spirit	Indecisiveness at moments of crisis
Completer/finisher	Painstaking, orderly, conscientious, anxious	A capacity for follow-through. Perfectionism	A tendency to worry about small things. A reluctance to 'let go'

Source: Team Management, Why Management Teams Succeed or Fail, Belbin, J, Heineman, 1981

through often failed to materialize. Using role analysis the team revised how it dealt with decisions. As each new decision was made it was written on a large flip chart and a name assigned as responsible for the next steps. The flip chart became the team's action minutes.

Using role analysis a team in one organization improved its choice of who to represent it at other meetings. If they wanted to stir things up and promote action they would send a Shaper, or even a Plant. If there was a need for someone to see through a detailed piece of work, maintaining good relations with everyone and being highly diplomatic, then it would send a Team or Company Worker.

Role analysis highlights the opportunity for team members to play several roles, particularly if there are only a few members. Also, if several people are competing, perhaps unconsciously, for the chairmanship role the power struggle may leave everyone feeling drained and demoralized. Using role analysis some members may see the value of modifying their natural chairmanship inclinations so that the team becomes more successful.

Role analysis has proved useful in many organizations, from ICI's paint division to social services departments, in focussing the team building effort. However, it is merely one approach amongst many.

Responsibility charting

It is sometimes helpful to clarify responsibilities within the organization. This can be particularly important when pursuing major change goals. Suppose, for example, a senior management team in a large retail chain of shops decides to unlock the value of the company's many high street properties. The team may assign different tasks to its members who individually or in groups implement the decision. Other people may also take part, contributing to the plan without necessarily being responsible for the work itself. What starts as a straightforward idea becomes increasingly complex involving many people. Clarifying accountability may be essential if the team and the change effort are to succeed. Responsibility charting helps obtain such clarification. While initially appearing cumbersome it has been widely used to:

- IDENTIFY who will do what on new decisions

- SHOW why decisions already taken have not been performed as intended

- IMPROVE how the team itself functions.

Responsibility charting requires a systematic approach and a willingness to debate vigorously those issues which it highlights. Though it can be useful to have someone outside the team to lead the charting exercise, it is not essential and managers can use it with a bit of practice.

The first step is to list all the types of decisions which have to be made. These are added down one side of a grid. Along the top is shown all the actors involved in the work as a whole (see Chart 25).

Chart 25

Responsibility chart

	R	– Responsibility (initiates)
	A-V	– Approval (right to veto)
	S	– Support (put resources against)
	I	– Inform (to be informed)

Actors → Decision ↓													

Source: Organizational Transactions: Managing Complex Change, Richard Beckhard and Reuben T. Harris, 1977, Addison-Wesley, Reading, MA. Figure 6.1

Charting proceeds by taking each decision and assigning one of four types of behaviour to each of the actors:

- *Responsibility (R)* – for initiating action to ensure that the decision is carried out. For example, it might be the managing director's responsibility to initiate an annual review of the organization's performance.

- *Approval or right to veto (A-V)* – a decision. For example, a

manager may have the right to approve or veto whether someone
takes part in a project initiated by someone else.

- **Support (S)** – provide logistical support and resources for the
  particular decision. For example, an accountant might be asked
  for information on some aspect of an agreed decision yet have
  no right to initiate action, exercise approval or veto it.

- **Inform (I)** – must be kept informed, with no right to influence
  the decision directly. For example, a training manager may have
  the right to be kept informed about new developments without
  a right to influence whether they proceed.

The work group debates each decision or action and against each
person assigns a responsibility using the appropriate letters – R,
A-V, S, and I – which are added to the grid. Anyone not participating at all in the decision is shown with a simple dash (-).

Assigning to each decision or task an appropriate responsibility
and person is revealing, though time consuming. Intense debate
may finally reveal that someone initially given a veto power is the
real decision maker. New understandings from charting responsibilities can ensure that changes required really do occur.

The system is most effective when the team insists on assigning
responsibility for particular items to only one person, even though
several may be needed to implement it. Similarly, on any one
decision or task only a few people should be granted the Approval-
Veto function, otherwise it will slow down or prevent implementation. Equally, by giving one person the right to approve or veto
most decisions there is a danger of creating bottlenecks or power
blockages.

The Support function (S) should be fully discussed as the person
who acquires this has a crucial role using resources in helping the
person ultimately responsible for the overall action.

Responsibility charting can be fun to do and bring to light
unexpected perspectives on the change effort. Like Circles of
Influence (see Chapter 6 on Power) it makes work on change more
systematic by stimulating new ways of tackling what seem
immovable blockages.

GUIDELINES

- GAIN support for the change effort through systematic team building

- DO NOT try to treat every work group as a formal team

- DISCOVER whether there are sound reasons for a group of people to work as a team

- CONSIDER who will lead the team building effort

- ENSURE that the group has time away from daily work pressures concentrating on team building

- USE existing team problems and tested methods for the team building effort

- ANALYSE what role each team member plays and the mix of roles within the team

- CONSIDER using responsibility charting to clarify the involvement of people in different decisions and actions.

Techniques
20. Verbal skills

Are you convincing and persuasive? How do you rate your verbal skills? To affect change in your organization good conversation skills are essential. There tends to be a direct relationship between a person's range of vocabulary and their likely status, power and prestige.

The more successful people are at ascending the management hierarchy the better they usually are at communicating in words and phrases. Though we usually equate communication with words and sounds we must never forget that these are always alongside and sometimes replaced by non-verbal messages. In fact, of the messages which human beings give each other, non-verbal messages predominate.

Chart 26

Human messages
The cues and signals we give

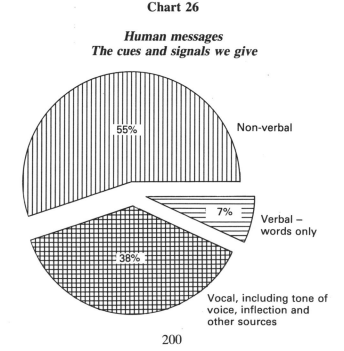

55% — Non-verbal

7% — Verbal – words only

38% — Vocal, including tone of voice, inflection and other sources

Some other research findings about verbal skills for managers are shown in Box 41.

Box 41

Some research findings on verbal skills

- The person who participates most actively in group activities where no one has been appointed or elected to lead is most likely to emerge as leader

- Oral communication abilities have been rated highest as a needed supervisory skill

- Industrial supervisors reported that they most wanted to learn 'how to sell ideas to my superior'

- When in a group, high status people did not perceive any loss of influence if they changed their opinions several times during a discussion

- More rapid promotion of managers was related to interpersonal competence

- The sheer quantity or percentage of time in interaction and working with others seems to contribute to one's success as a leader

- There is a direct relationship between status, power and prestige and a person's range of vocabulary

Influencing change involves persuading others to accept new ideas and a different *status quo*. Verbal skills and an understanding of non-verbal cues are important for obtaining that acceptance. Verbal skills include those shown in Box 42. Rate yourself from one to five on how effective you are at each of these 20 skills. Better still, ask a colleague who knows you well to rate you. Add up your scores and if you obtain a score of less than 85 read on!

Most talking is impromptu and open to misunderstandings. Words are misheard, intonations misinterpreted, something unintended is conveyed. For instance, if you receive a note from the trade union asking what you are going to do about a pay anomaly there is time to analyse it and send a considered response. Faced with the same question in a management-union meeting and pressure to respond, you may betray your ignorance or become committed to unnecessary action.

Managers are generally better at talking than listening. Yet the problems associated with change frequently stem from too little listening. It is dangerous to assume that those on the receiving end

Box 42

Verbal skills managers need

- Listen actively
- Negotiate
- Say No
- Deal with personal criticism
- Present proposals and sell ideas
- Disagree without being aggressive or rude
- Offer praise
- Criticize constructively
- Contribute to meetings
- Make a formal speech in front of strangers
- Argue logically
- Sound committed
- Summarize accurately what others have said
- Avoid interrupting
- Chair meetings
- Redefine problems as opportunities
- Obtain information that people are trying to conceal
- Use questions without sounding inquisitorial
- State complicated things simply
- Handle differences of opinion

---

usually understand us – mostly they are failing to understand. Research into listening by the Sperry Company found success rates of communication of only 25 per cent. In other words, three-quarters of communications are not really understood.

Courses on negotiating, chairing meetings, making presentations, giving a speech and so on all teach aspects of verbal skills. Such skills make you a better all round manager and are essential in any change effort which you lead. Some verbal skills can be learned from reading and practising in situations where making mistakes does not matter. Some basics are covered in the rest of this chapter.

Non-verbals

Alongside verbal interaction is the vast amount of non-verbal communication made with eyes, heads, limbs and other bodily gestures. While the verbal channel mainly conveys information, the non-verbal channel negotiates interpersonal attitudes, and in some cases is a direct substitute for a verbal message.

Understanding people by looking at them and adapting your verbal response appropriately is an art with a long history of folklore and half truth. The main lesson from research is:

**A single non-verbal gesture is seldom
enough from which to draw conclusions.**

Watch for several linked gestures rather than a single event. Once
you start noticing them you will begin using them to tailor your
every day verbal approach. For instance, what would you conclude
if your boss listens with one hand on his cheek, index finger pointing
upwards, another finger covering his mouth and the thumb supporting the chin, and his legs crossed? Studies of non-verbal cues
suggest that these combined signals reveal: 'I don't like what you
are saying and I disagree with you.'

You can adapt your verbal response by translating the unspoken
language. If you notice that someone adopts your own general
bodily posture, for example, such as leaning forward or sitting with
hands in a like manner, it can signal that you are succeeding in
your persuasion efforts.

Most managers know something about eye movement and
contact and how it encourages or deters talking. It also signals:
'I'm glad to see you' or 'I know that you are here.' For instance,
a senior manager may pass through to his own room giving a nod,
half smile or wave matched with a brief moment of eye contact to
recognize and acknowledge each person in the outer office.

Verbal skills thus include knowing about active listening, body
language, use of personal space, eye contact and so on. Freud
concluded that: '. . . no mortal can keep a secret. If his lips are
silent he chatters with his finger tips, betrayal oozes out of him at
every pore.'

Conflict resolution

Challenging the *status quo* often causes conflict. To handle change
well managers need the verbal skills to deal with conflict situations.
These involve discussion in which you separate:

- Problems from solutions

- Facts from opinions

- Feelings from logical reasoning.

A framework for tackling conflict situations can be helpful, particularly if you are the kind of person who finds conflict unpleasant. The main conflict management steps are shown in Box 43.

Box 43

The steps for managing conflict

1   CONFRONT the conflict – acknowledge to yourself that a conflict exists; communicate to the other party that there is a conflict; assert positively your wants, wishes and preferences

2   UNDERSTAND the other person's position – listen; give feedback and restate their position to show you understand; use 'I' statements rather than 'you' blame/language

3   DEFINE the problem(s) – try and reach a mutually acceptable definition of the problem; avoid a combative approach at this stage; acknowledge your strengths and vulnerabilities; be prepared to change if necessary; be honest

4   SEARCH for and evaluate alternative solutions – collaborate to obtain a mutually acceptable solution; separate creating alternatives from evaluating them; solve the most manageable problems first; jointly ask: 'which solution looks best' not 'which do I prefer?'

5   AGREE on and implement the best solution(s) – treat the agreement like a contract, seek great clarity and specificity; state who will do what by when etc

Some of the blocks to sorting out conflict situations may also stem directly from a manager's lack of verbal skills such as those shown in Box 44.

Questions

Senior managers generally pride themselves on their ability to ask the right questions. Questions steer conversation and direct interactions. They can indeed be powerful and should be used sparingly. Since most interactions contain some kind of questioning you should become familiar with the main types of questions, shown in Box 45.

Asking a question is less effective if the person is unsure why you are asking it. For example, if your boss asks: 'Where were you yesterday?' it could either be followed by: 'because I wanted to invite you to lunch,' or 'because I couldn't find you and had to deal with a problem which was your responsibility.' Questions thus spring from a variety of directions or motives and if those on the receiving end are unsure about these they may be defensive,

Box 44

Blocks to resolving conflicts

- WRONG LANGUAGE – combatative rather than collaborative verbal and non-verbal communications

- NOT CONFRONTING – failing to acknowledge differences; not raising issues; raising them in an aggressive way and creating defensiveness

- POOR TIMING – you talk of conflict when either you or they are not ready to acknowledge or handle it

- EXCESS TALKING – not listening to the other's point of view; being too ready to criticise; leaving the other person no space to express feelings

- MISUSE OF LANGUAGE – 'You-blame' rather than 'I' statements; emotive words like 'you idiot', 'that's crazy' or other put downs; repeating your views too much and appearing domineering

- VOCAL EXCESSES – dominating with a loud voice; frightening with a shrill voice; chilling with a cold voice

- LACK OF OPENNESS – you fail to state the real reason for the conflict; you lie; you suppress information particularly if it is unfavourable to your case; not admitting negative or positive feelings you have for the other party

- POOR ANGER CONTROL – your own or other people's

---

guarded or aggressive. What happens when you ask one question is aggravated by a barrage of questions. Like trouble, questions seldom come singly and escalate with each succeeding answer.

Questions can work well when you explain their purpose. If you are unwilling to explain why you need to know something then your communications with others will not be considered open or helpful. If delivered effectively, so that the other person understands why you are asking them, questions:

Offer scope to provide general information
or
elicit specific answers.

The first of these is a divergent approach, opening up opportunities for communication. Divergent type questions steer the conversation away from a single response or specific reply. If you want to explore a situation, discover what people are thinking, develop new ideas, then a divergent approach using open ended questions, redefining questions and ones which pose no threat are the best way of achieving results.

Box 45

Questions that managers ask

- CLOSED QUESTIONS seek precise short brief information: 'Do you have a degree?; 'What is the sales turnover?'; 'Have you met Mr Jones?'

- OPEN ENDED QUESTIONS – encourage the other person to feel there are no conversational boundaries: 'How are things going?'; 'Tell me about your present job'; 'What's it like working here?'

- DIRECT QUESTIONS – demand more information than simple closed questions because they assert your authority and right to know something: 'Why did that happen?'; 'Who is involved in this'; 'What authority did you have to overspend?'

- INDIRECT QUESTIONS – gain information obliquely: 'When are you going to leave the company' may be less effective than 'What are your personal career plans over the next few years?' Or, 'Do you have a contingency plan' may be less effective than 'How would we cope in an emergency?'

- HYPERBOLE QUESTIONS – provoke the other person, perhaps to a denial, an admission or to offer some refutation: 'Is it true that you're going broke?' 'Heavens no! But I do admit that we're having a problem with debtor accounts.'

- REDEFINING QUESTIONS – restate a problem or a situation to help break an impasse or deal with conflict: 'Would you agree that another way of looking at it is . . .?

- RHETORICAL QUESTIONS – make statements in a way that indicate that no answer is required, either because it is obvious or not expected: 'If that is the annual loss what hope is there for the firm's survival?'; 'Surely we shouldn't just sit and do nothing about it?'

- LEADING QUESTIONS – suggest what the answer should be: 'Do you accept that you were negligent?'; 'Would you agree that . . .'

The second approach is a convergent one in which questions narrow down answers towards a single target area. You are less interested in exploration and more concerned with gaining hard information quickly. Closed, direct and leading questions all tend to steer the conversation into relatively narrow channels.

Next time you ask a question think about whether you are opening up or closing down the range of possibilities for an answer.

If you enjoy using questions, use them sparingly and avoid a gun slinger style of delivery.

Assertiveness

Assertiveness is when you insist that your views, feelings and needs are considered. This implies standing up for your rights and handling other people's undesirable behaviour.

A right is something to which you are entitled. In any situation you have rights. For instance, a manager has the right to expect and receive typing of the required standard and to show mistakes to the typist. The typist has the right to have these mistakes mentioned in a reasonable manner without being humiliated or feeling under personal attack. Asserting your rights and respecting the rights of others are inextricably linked with achieving change.

To influence change managers must be seen as positive and constructive people who are meeting both their own needs and those of other people in the organization. Being positive and constructive, often in the face of resistance and other negative factors, means being assertive.

Assertiveness is essential because it encourages assertion in others so that people are more likely to continue working with rather than against you. Considerable evidence exists to show that lack of assertiveness and aggression stem from low self esteem (what you think about yourself and how you evaluate your worth as a person).

When you consider yourself to be competent, significant, likeable and successful you have high self esteem. With low self esteem you will be anxious and uncertain and you will communicate this in the way you talk and behave, making it harder to convince others about the need for change.

Assertion is also standing up for your own rights, needs and beliefs without violating those of other people. People behaving assertively do the kind of things shown in Box 46. Next time you listen to a conversation at work try classifying it into whether it is: assertive, non-assertive or aggressive. As with recognizing and intepreting non-verbal cues, it requires practice. Raising your own personal consciousness about what is happening will improve your effectiveness.

When you are introducing change you must constantly ask people for help, and be competent at handling situations where people disagree, resist and generally express doubts about what is being proposed. Thus two crucial skills are: making requests and disagreeing without aggression.

By making requests assertively you seek help in a way that makes people want to assist, without feeling that they have no choice.

Box 46

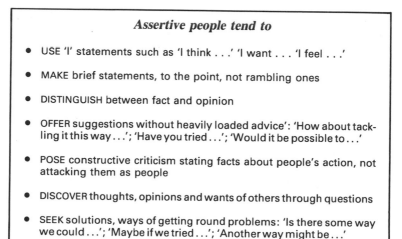

Likewise, you must cope with the many situations where there is some disagreement about what should be done. Box 47 offers hints on making requests and disagreeing without aggression.

Box 47

> **Hints on making requests and disagreeing without aggression**
>
> | Making requests | Disagreeing without aggression |
> |---|---|
> | NEVER apologize for seeking help | STATE clearly that you disagree |
> | BE direct | EXPRESS doubts constructively |
> | KEEP it short | USE 'I' statements |
> | DO NOT try to justify yourself | CHANGE your opinion in the light |
> | GIVE a reason for your request | of new information |
> | NEVER sell the request with | GIVE reasons for your |
> | flattery or promises | disagreement |
> | AVOID playing on people's | SAY exactly what you disagree |
> | friendship or good nature | with |
> | DO NOT take a refusal personally | RECOGNIZE other people's point |
> | RESPECT the other person's right | of view |
> | to say no | |

These are just some of the assertiveness techniques which you can adopt.

Feedback

Feedback is another easily acquired verbal skill and a powerful tool during the change effort as you seek to discover how to persuade people to do things and uncover reasons for resistance. Helpful feedback includes the kinds shown in Box 48.

Box 48

Helpful feedback is

- Descriptive not evaluative

- Specific not general

- Relevant to the self-perceived needs of the receiver

- Desired by the receiver, not imposed

- Timely and in context

- Usable, concerned with things over which the receiver has some control

Top ten hints

Charles Margerison, Professor of Management at the University of Queensland, has worked with many managers to improve their verbal skills. He offers a useful ten-point guide on conversational control:

- ***Listen for the cues and clues*** – key words and phrases indicating points of interest or concern; do not change the topic of conversation when people use 'I', 'me' or 'my' and adjectives showing they are annoyed, worried, happy and so on.

- ***Learn to move from being problem centred to solution centred and back again*** – stay in the problem centred area until you know enough about causes.

- ***Manage your conversational time*** – prevent conversations becoming fixated with one time dimension such as the past; deal with the present and the future.

- ***Take a personal interest in permissions and territory*** – permission is about seeking agreement to discuss certain matters, directly or indirectly: 'I'd like to talk to you about this note you wrote to me'. Territory is when people claim something for their own: 'I'm not prepared to discuss that'; 'I'm sorry, these minutes only go to members of the project team.'

- **Seek the win/win option as the first priority** – best conversations are those where both participants emerge winners having gained something.

- **Manage both facts and opinions** – never allow one to dominate at the expense of the other; where you have many opinions seek facts; if you have a lot of facts seek opinions.

- **Convert the verbals to the visuals** – give people an opportunity to see and hear by presenting information visually.

- **Give accurate summaries, understand before you judge** – summarize regularly and accurately to gain agreement.

- **Assert yourself** – stand up for what you want without being aggressive; understand and recognize what the other person has said, then be positive about putting forward what you want.

- **Emphasize the positives** – watch out for the negative tendencies in your conversations; get people thinking about 'how to' rather than 'how not to'.

These points are explained in more detail in Margerison's book on *Conversational Skills for Managers* (see References and Further Reading at the end of the book).

Finally, taking the last of these hints a bit further, have you tried measuring your 'but quotient'? Someone with an open mind tends to have a low BQ, close to zero. The word 'but' is a truly powerful negator. Its negative effect is far greater than you intend, on others and yourself. Reduce your BQ by using the word 'and', without making it sound like but!

GUIDELINES

- WATCH non-verbal behaviour; look for linked gestures; never rely on just one to interpret meaning

- HANDLE conflict by:
    Separating problems from solutions, facts from opinions and logical reasoning from feelings;
    Confronting it;
    Understanding the other person's position;
    Defining the problem(s);
    Looking for, evaluating and implementing the best solutions(s)

- USE questions sparingly

- ASK questions in a non-threatening way by explaining why you are asking them

- ASSERT yourself by standing up for your rights and dealing with others' undesirable behaviours

- MAKE requests and disagree without aggression

- USE the Margerison ten-point guide for conversational control

- MINIMIZE your 'But' quotient.

References and further reading

Chapter 1 – Models
WHYTE W F. 'Models for Building and Changing Organizations', in *The Management of Change and Conflict* by Thomas M J and Bennis W G, Penguin, 1972, pp 227–238

TICHEY N. 'The Essentials of Strategic Change Management', *Journal of Business Strategy*, Spring 1983

LIMERICK D and CUNNINGHAM B. 'Management Development: The Fourth Blueprint', *Journal of Management Development*, Volume 6, No 1, 1987

HUCZYNSKI H. *Encyclopedia of Organizational Change Methods*, Gower Publishing Company, 1987, pp 5–15

Chapter 2 – Leadership
SAYLES L. *Leadership, What Effective Managers Really Do and How They Do It*, McGraw Hill, 1979

STOGDILL'S *Handbook of Leadership*, ed Bass B M, Free Press, 1981

NICHOLLS, J R. 'A new approach to situational leadership', *Leadership and Organization Development Journal*, Vol 6, 1985

TICHEY N and DEVANNA M A. *The Transformational Leader*, John Wiley, 1986

Chapter 3 – Vision and values
TICKEY N and DEVANNA M A. 'Creating A Motivating Vision', in *The Transformational Leader*, John Wiley, 1986, pp 90–147

BLOCK P. *The Empowered Manager: Positive Political Skills at Work*, Jossey-Bass Publishers, 1987, pp 99–129

PLANT R. *Managing Change and Making It Stick*, Fontana, 1987, pp 73–86

SCULLEY J. *Odyssey*, William Collins Sons and Company, 1987, pp 323–328

PETERS T. *Thriving on Chaos*, Macmillan, 1988, pp 398–408

Chapter 4 – Commitment
MARTIN P and NICHOLS J. *Creating a Committed Workforce*, Institute of Personnel Management, 1987

TICHEY N and DEVANNA M A. 'Mobilising Commitment', in *The Transformational Leader*, John Wiley, 1986, pp 149–182

WATERMAN Jr. *The Renewal Factor*, Bantam Press, 1988, pp 293–312

Chapter 5 – Simplify
KANTER R. *The Change Masters*, Geo Allen and Unwin, 1984, pp 148
PETERS T and WATERMAN R. 'Experimenting Organisations', in *In Search of Excellence*, 1982, Harper and Row 1982, pp 150–154, 310–317

Chapter 6 – Power and influence
KOTTER J. *Power in Management*, AMACON, 1979
WATERMAN Jr R. *The Renewal Factor*, Bantam Press, 1988, pp 199–212

Chapter 7 – Resistance to change
HULTMAN K. *The Path of Least Resistance*, Learning Concepts, Texas, 1979
TICHEY N and DEVANNA M A. *The Transformational Leader*, John Wiley, 1986, pp 59–86

Chapter 8 – Planning strategic change
QUINN J. 'Strategic Change: Logical Incrementalism', *Sloan Management Review*, Vol 20, No 1, 1978
KANTER R. *The Change Masters*, Geo Allen and Unwin, 1984, pp 294–296
SCULLEY J. *Odyssey*, William Collins Sons and Company, 1987, pp 292–297
PUMPIN C. *The Essence of Corporate Strategy*, Gower Press, 1987

Chapter 9 – Actions sequence
No recommendations

Chapter 10 – Experimenting
NOLAN V. *Open to Change*, MCB Publications, 1981, pp 14–34
PETERS T and WATERMAN R. 'Experimenting Organisations', in *In Search of Excellence*, Harper and Row, 1982, pp 134–150

Chapter 11 – Participative decision making
NEUMANN J. *Enhancing Willingness to Participate*. Publication No.811182, Vol. 49–04A. University Microfilms International, Ann Arbor, Michigan, 1988
Putting Participation into Practice, ed Guest D, and Knight K, Gower Press, 1979
GILLIES E. *Employee Participation and Decision Making Structures*, Australian Government Publishing Service, Canberra, 1983
GILBERT J. 'Human factors – the Key to Getting a Competitive Edge', *Human Participation*, Winter 1986/7
Priority Decision System (PDS): supplied by Work Science Associates, 26 Southwood Lawn Road, London N6 5SF
WATERMAN Jr. *The Renewal Factor*, Bantam Press, 1988, pp 84–90

Chapter 12 – Stress
KAHN R L etc. *The Management of Organisational Stress*, Wiley, 1964, pp 375–98
WHITE G. *Managing Stress in Organisational Change*, WRU Occasional Paper 31, 1984
CRANWELL-WARD J. *Managing Stress*, Gower Publishing, 1987

Chapter 13 – Outside agents

KAKABADSE A. *How to Use Consultants*, MCB Press, Vol 4, No 1, 1983
Seeking Help From Management Consultants by Cabinet Office (Management and Personnel Office), 1985

Chapter 14 – Tracking

WARMINGTON *et al*. 'The Evaluation of Success in Change', in *Organisation Behaviour and Performance, an Open Systems Approach to Change*, pp 188–194
PORRAS J. *Stream Analysis*, Addison-Wesley, OD Series, 1987

Chapter 15 – Force field analysis

FORDYCE J R and WELLS R. *Managing With People*, Addison-Wesley, pp 106–8
PAGE D, JONES L. *Planned Change Through Force Field Analysis*, Castlevale Ltd, 3 Station Parade, Balham SW12 9AZ

Chapter 16 – Sensing

FORDYCE J R and WELLS R. *Managing With People*, Addison-Wesley, pp 143–146
JONES E J. 'The Sensing Interview', in *The 1973 Annual Handbook for Group Facilitators*, University Associates, California, pp 213–224
PLANT R. *Managing Change and Making It Stick*, Fontana, 1987, pp 66–72

Chapter 17 – Mundane tools of change

PETERS T. 'Symbols, Patterns and Settings: An Optimistic Case for Getting Things Done, *Organisational Dynamics*, Autumn 1978

Chapter 18 – Management by walking about

PETERS T and WATERMAN R. 'Experimenting Organisations', *In Search of Excellence*, Harper and Row, 1982
HALBERSTAM D. *The Reckoning*, Bloomsbury Publishing Ltd, 1986, pp 209

Chapter 19 – Team building

GAWLINSKI G. *Planning Together, The Art of Effective Teamwork*, Bedford Square Press, 1988
WOODCOCK M. *Team Development Manual*, Gower Publishing, 1979
WOODCOCK M and FRANCIS D, *Organisation Development Through Team Building*, Gower Publishing, 1981
BELBIN M. *Management Teams, Why They Succeed or Fail*, Heinemann Publishing, 1981
WATERMAN Jr. *The Renewal Factor*, Bantam Press, 1988, pp 179–183; 207–212

Chapter 20 – Verbal skills

NOLAN V. *Open to Change*, MCB Publications, 1981, pp 59–61, 65

TORRINGTON D. *Face to Face in Management*, Prentice Hall International Inc, 1982

BLACK K. *Assertiveness at Work*, McGraw Hill Book Company (UK) Ltd, 1982

NELSON-JONES R. *Human Relationship Skills*, Cassell Educational Ltd, East Sussex, 1986, pp 106–162; 221–248

PEASE A. *Body Language*, Sheldon Press, 1986

MARGERISON C. *Conversational Control for Managers*, Mercury Books Division, W H Allen and Co, 1987

Index